The Biggest BUT
in the World

Natalie K. Hodge

DEDICATION

To my dad, Rufus Hodge, who taught me to laugh until I cry and cry until I laugh.

CONTENTS

Acknowledgments   i

Prologue   1

1   This Very Minute   7

2   Your Big Ole But   14

3   Self-Centered vs. Centered Self   24

4   Get Over You Then Get Into You   30

5   Mission and Movements   40

6   Joy Thieves   48

7   There's a Blessing in the Storm   57

8   Once You Know You – Grow You   64

9   When Buts Attack   70

10   But Busters   77

11   Buy Your Own Stock   84

12   But Paralysis   91

13   Bye But   96

ACKNOWLEDGMENTS

I am eternally grateful to my partner, Joseph Billups, who supported me in all aspects of this process from reviewing book cover designs to carrying bags to photo shoots.

My sincerest gratitude goes out to my mother, Judy Hodge, who has supported every great and terrible idea I've ever had. Thank you for believing in my crazy visions.

To my entire family, whether by blood or the bond of eternal friendship, your love through the years sustained me. You are my angels. This project is a manifestation of the incredible moments we've had together. I've learned so much from all of you.
THANK YOU!

Special thanks to the amazing community of people who rallied around me in the making and marketing of this book. Many of you shared your expertise and time with no expectation of compensation:
Myra Moore, Editor
Dionte Smith, Marketing and Promotions
D'Colby Green-McNary, Marketing and Promotions
Dina Six, Producer
Elizamar Martinez, Photographer
Mimi Miller, Hairstylist
Adriana Loza, Make-up Artist

PROLOGUE

The idea for this book came to me while I was on a completely packed airplane on my way to my friends Alyssa and Josh's wedding in Portland, Oregon. Believe it or not, I was quite the sight as the world's oldest flower girl. The start of the trip, however, was not all roses. I arrived at LAX right on time in my mind. I wasn't aware that construction to the terminal would extend the check-in process an additional 45 minutes. I watched the clock as the line inched along. It was my boarding time and I was nowhere near the TSA checkpoint.

I made a decision that there was nothing I could do about the slow moving line or my plane leaving without me. I committed to myself that it was going to be an amazing trip regardless of this snaffoo. I smiled and sang to myself as I waited. I didn't gallop off to the gate with my shoes half on and my purse spilling over as I normally might have. If it were meant for me to catch the flight, I would be able to do it without mowing down the elderly or small children along the way. The TSA line was so long, the flight should have been in the air anyway, so all need to rush was completely eliminated.

To my surprise, when I arrived at the gate, the flight had been delayed. The final boarding call announcement had just been made as I approached. "What luck?" I thought. I missed all of the fighting for position that happens when you wait to board the plane. I moseyed right up and immediately the gate attendant asked if she could move me to another seat since there was a larger woman in the seat next to the one assigned to me. She said it would probably be more comfortable to sit somewhere else.

Score! This was another awesome gift from the universe. The gate attendant was already thinking about my comfort. I boarded the plane and found a free overhead bin by my seat, which happened to be in a completely empty row. The world was my oyster and I knew it was because I made a conscious decision to be positive. I sat feeling very proud of myself and excited about what might happen next. Perhaps, I'd find a winning lottery ticket someone left behind as a bookmark in the SkyMall magazine. I stretched out over the empty neighboring seat and thumbed through the seat pocket reading material as we awaited the closing of the cabin doors.

Just when my attitude teetered on the borderline of smug, a couple with two small children raced onto the plane. I knew there were no other seats available so they had to be coming back to my sweet retreat. The smallest child was no more than one and began to cry loudly as soon as they boarded. The older son was big enough to walk and ask 10,000 questions a minute. I could hear him talking and whining every time the infant took a breath between screams. The parents looked completely unraveled as the troop bumped every seat along the path to the back of the aircraft.

The mom sat with the screaming baby on the seat beside me. I looked over and remembered the lesson I'd learned earlier in line. It doesn't matter what the circumstance is, you can make a choice about how you respond. I decided I was going to sleep. I didn't care that the baby was nearly drooling on my arm as she screamed in aggravation or that the young son wanted to play with everything until he actually got it into his hands. It didn't matter. I was intent on sleeping. I closed my eyes and made it happen. Somehow, some way, I was able to doze off. While in my nap haze, I started to think about everything that could have prevented me from getting to the wedding. There were so many points along the way that I had not previously considered as possible trip derailments.

Inevitably, that's life. There are many situations that can keep us from getting where we want to go, but ultimately we are in control of how we respond to all of them. While I wasn't in control of the airport construction, long line or crying baby, I was in charge of my attitude. That attitude helped me to have a great flight in spite of all the rest. I won, because I didn't let the *buts* of the experience take over. "I made the flight, *BUT* there was a long line." "I had a comfortable seat, *BUT* there was a crying baby beside me." Those *buts* don't have to be a part of the story. They contribute nothing to the value of your life experience and in most cases; they actually keep you from experiencing life to the fullest.

This book is about eliminating the *buts* in your life starting with the biggest *BUT* in the world - the one you allow to keep you from your incredible destiny.

Introduction to But-ology

If you've never heard of a but-alogist, just wait; they'll be all the rage next year. But-alogists are experts in the study of excuse making and excuse resolution. But-ology is a blossoming field and I am certain book stores all over the world will have to expand their shelf space to accommodate the influx of new material. In the coming months, colleges and universities across the country will be scrambling to find but-ologists to teach courses. But-ologists will hit the talk show circuit. Shortly thereafter, we'll have a reality show where several of us who were previously strangers will live in a house on a deserted island where we have to pitch our life changing ideas to sharks. #RealButTank

For the record, although this book is filled with humor, my commitment to but-ology is very serious. My training in the field started at an early age. I grew up in a family where excuses were not tolerated. Before I could part my lips to say, "But I…" someone was there to shut me down. I learned the ropes in a very adult world with only a few cousins close to my age and tons of great aunts and uncles who were in their golden years. Even though I got plenty of attention, no one had time to baby me.

I was so lucky to have great parents. They both played a role in holding me accountable. My dad had a particularly interesting style, as he didn't always adhere to traditional parenting practices. Dad believed in raising me as a very independent little person. He would often allow me to govern myself and make decisions on my own. For example, I once asked him what dog food tasted like. He said, "Try it and see." He watched as I ate several pellets of dry dog food. Lesson learned - it was disgusting. He was there to supervise my experiment and he never had to worry about me sneaking back into the bag for a snack.

There were countless scenarios that took place on my weekends and summer vacations with dad where I learned that life is about making choices, accepting consequences and then adjusting behaviors if consequences were unfavorable. I also learned that if you want an edible hot dog, it's probably best not to cook it with a blowtorch. It was a very colorful childhood!

Like most kids, I was no angel. However, my family made it very challenging to get over on them at anytime. Everyone slept with one eye opened, even the dog. Making up an acceptable excuse for poor grades or poor behavior was a feat. I was determined though and unfortunately, at some point, I became adept at creatively avoiding responsibility. I always knew better and when one of my well-constructed excuses fell apart, they were there to hold me accountable.

For many years, there was a tug of war happening inside me. One part of me responded to challenges and setbacks in a productive and positive way, while the other enacted a full-fledged blame game. Even as I had begun my profession of helping other people reach their desired goals in life, I struggled with committing fully to my own. On so many occasions, I allowed stinking thinking to take me off course. My skills for excuse making were incredible, so much so that I fully believed my own bologna.

Life continued to happen and eventually I tired of living outside my potential. I started a personal development journey where I spent hundreds of hours reading, listening to and watching material that taught me that what life had to offer was limitless if I would just get out of my own way. As a result, I made a lifelong commitment to helping others create success regardless of the given circumstances.

In my new universe, there is no space for buts - only guts! My vision is that the work I do in the But-ology field will help people all over the world identify and discard the excuses that prevent them from having their best lives now. The challenge is that, I, too, am a work in progress. I will expose many of my current struggles in this book. I share them because I've read many self-help books that leave me feeling like I have so much work to do in order to gain the same level of success as the author. I may be really motivated when I put the book down but there's often a delay making the life changes recommended. The weight of my own imperfection is so heavy sometimes, I can hardly move.

I know now, that achieving success in spite of your *but*, happens when you start immediately. This is not a process where you wait until you've gotten your life together to begin your transformation. This is a "do it now" book.

Finally, this book is strategically formatted to attack your *buts* as you read. There are assessments called "Self-Checks," in most chapters to help you personally connect with the material. The length is designed to maximize your progress and minimize your "it's going to take too much time" *but*. The tone of the book is set up based on how I would talk to a person in one of my success coaching sessions. My style is very much like an auntie. I hold folks accountable, but I'm absolutely not a drill sergeant. Ultimately, this is your journey, so regardless of how much intention I incorporate into the structure of the book; only you can determine what you get out of it.

1 THIS VERY MINUTE

This very minute you are either moving toward the life you want or moving away from it. There is no in between, no pauses and no pit stops. Either you are progressing or digressing. If you are reading this book to get a stern butt kicking to assist you in getting your *but* in order, then congratulations you are moving toward your ultimate goals. If you are reading this book to avoid doing what you know is necessary to get you to your goals, you are moving away from your personal and professional paradise. If you are reading this in a bookstore, proceed to the counter to make the purchase, then figure out where you land.

While my intellectual talent does not lie in the sciences, one of my favorite classes in high school was Physics. This is mainly because Mr. Brown, my Physics teacher, made everything so tangible. I didn't particularly like science or think I was good at it, but his lessons made plain some high level concepts. I thoroughly enjoyed his lectures on energy. As I recall, there is potential energy and kinetic energy. For those of you non-science heads who didn't have Mr. Brown, potential energy is a force that is not yet activated. The object or entity can move into the kinetic form of energy, but something else has to happen first. Kinetic energy is when an object or entity is in motion.

This book is intended to move you from potential energy to kinetic energy in the plainest terms possible. I'm taking a lesson from Mr. Brown's teaching style, although I vow this will be my last science reference. Just getting through that paragraph almost turned my kinetic energy back to potential. What I'm candidly sharing from my personal experiences with all levels of success and failure is enclosed in these pages to inspire you to take action. This heartfelt share means absolutely nothing, if you get to the last page then go right back to watching a marathon of episodes from your favorite television show.

More than anything, I want to dialogue with readers in the future and find out what they are doing as a result of reading, *The Biggest BUT in the World.* It's great if readers fall in love with the book, however, it's more important that they get into kinetic mode. If someone says, "I hated that book, but I'm on my path to success," I'll take it.

MAKE A COMMITMENT RIGHT NOW to use whatever nuggets you can find in these pages to change your life and change the lives of those around you. For most of you, this isn't your first personal development book. If you've read as many as I have, you know how high they can take you in your evolved thinking and how low you can go once the initial high wears off. Slap yourself right now! (Not crazy, abusive hard) Just give yourself a little tap on the cheek or the knee and say, "I commit, this very minute to doing and not just saying, to moving and not just sitting and to living and not just being."

This very minute is the most important minute of your life as it is the only minute you can change. The minutes to come are not here to contour and the minutes already gone cannot be altered. Whether good, bad or ugly - this very minute is all you have. At some point, if you're like me, you'll start thinking about all the minutes you've wasted. If you have a good memory, you will waste more minutes and even hours reflecting on stupid projects, lovers, internet searches, television shows, movies, shopping expeditions, hobbies, etc on which you've wasted time. When that happens, give yourself another light slap. (If you are making bruises with these slaps, you've gone too far.) These playful, and for those of you who can't handle the physicality, metaphorical slaps are just "wake up" points. Remember, you can't change what has already been and wasting time lamenting it, just leaves you less time to enjoy all life has to offer.

Skippers should proceed with caution too. *Skippers* are people who read one line of something and skip ahead to a wildly imaginative land of prosperity and unicorns. If you've daydreamed about success three times already before getting to this paragraph, give yourself a gentle real or metaphorical slap. STOP! You can hardly get anything done in life because you are living in a fantasy world. You're missing real life's most important moments in the land of the clouds.

Am I bashing dreamers? Heavens no! I dream with the best of the best, baby. I can out dream a person in a coma, but I know that a dream with no action will forever live in your head. At some point, we all have to focus on making the dream a reality. If that never happens, the beautiful invention, innovation, solution, creative work or life changing process will never be born. The dream will never benefit anyone, not even the dreamer. When you are operating from a perspective where you value, this very minute, you grant yourself the opportunity to daydream or positively reflect for a limited time before taking action.

The other important item to note as you are learning the best use of this very minute is that you should love it. Some of you will automatically reject the idea of loving this minute. You may have been drawn to this book because you feel terribly out of alignment. There's a poop storm raining down on you and all you could think to do is try to find a little guidance here. The fact that you had the wherewithal to seek help and the means to secure this indicates something is going right in your life. Two wins are better than none and every championship team on the planet had to have two wins before taking home a trophy.

Love this very minute. If that is an issue for you, stop reading momentarily and take time to write down as many things as possible for which you are grateful. While I am not the genius who came up with the idea of writing gratitude lists, I am so thankful to the person who did. They work incredibly well for me especially when I feel like the world is plotting against me. There are some days when I've had to start my list with "breathing." You know times are tough when just being alive is all you can come up with initially. The key is not to stop at breathing, but to push harder to write a few more things down. If you're reading this, don't take your literacy for granted. A quick look at illiteracy numbers in the U.S. alone will shock you, but also help you to realize, you have one more thing for which to be thankful.

Once you are committed to loving this very minute, no matter what, you can move forward with your next steps. If you still have some type of internal hold up, put this book down and figure out how to move past it. Maybe there is another book that's a good starting point and then you can return to this riveting read. This is not constructed to teach you how to love yourself or the life you have created. It's designed to get you moving and motivated. If you've fallen out of love with you, there's no clever antic or personal story I could share to get you to a space of productivity. The foundation for creating any positive change is love.

The *But* of Procrastination

This is just as good a time as any to address our first *but*. It will absolutely rear its ugly head as you start your transformation. This book would have been written a year ago were it not for this *but*. It is the *but* of procrastination and if you let it, procrastination will keep you from completing this very short book.

Procrastination wages war against this very minute. It convinces you that delaying action is acceptable. It lulls you into thinking time is of no consequence and that you have an unlimited supply of it from which to work. Procrastination turns minute delays into hours and hour delays into days until eventually, your goal becomes a memory.

While procrastination delays the process of you receiving great things in your life, it also gives challenges a steroid injection. Here's an example of how it works. You have an appointment scheduled for 4:00 p.m. at a location 20 minutes from your house. Because you just had to see the results of the lie detector test on your favorite talk show, you don't leave until 3:45 p.m. Road construction and rush hour traffic tack on another 10 minutes to your drive time. Now you know you're going to be late. As you're rushing to reach your destination, you park in a restricted parking area. After your appointment, you return to your car and find a very ugly gift situated underneath the wiper blade. It's a big fat $100 parking ticket due at the end of the month.

You could close out this unpleasant chain of events by immediately paying the ticket and learning the lesson. However, you are so aggravated every time you see the ticket that you throw it in your desk drawer. Life goes on and soon you get a letter notifying you that the ticket is now $200. A rage bubbles inside you as you look at your bank account and realize you don't even have the money to pay the ticket if you wanted to. It will just have to wait until the funds are available. Months pass and one evening when you're wrapping up a night on the town, you walk back to a parking space where your car once sat. Your precious vehicle has been towed and your *but* was definitely the reason.

"*But* I can do it later" and "*but* I don't have time right now" can create untold obstacles for you. Small challenges are magnified. They create a number of delays that ripple through the rest of your life. You could have paid the parking ticket in a couple of minutes, but because you procrastinated, hours and maybe even days have to be invested in ironing out the whole situation. The money you spend to get the car out of the tow yard may have been earmarked for a much needed vacation or an investment. Instead of having access to it for something positive in your life, you're cleaning up a procrastination mess.

Living by the principle of this very minute keeps you connected to the activities in your life that are priorities. You know what needs to happen right now and you also know when to strategically delay action. Before you run off and tell the bank you are strategically delaying your mortgage payment, finish reading this book. In order for any of the helpful hints inside to work, you must be operating from a place of noble intentions. Hard core procrastinators will use "strategic delay" as their new slogan for not taking care of business.

Sometimes procrastinators aren't operating from a place of limited consciousness. Often there are well thought out reasons for delays in action. Many of the people I've mentored over the years have fallen into the pitfall of procrastinating because they are waiting for the optimal time. While there is a time and place for everything, there isn't an optimal time for anything. Your life will always have some complication that needs to be worked through. For as many reasons as you can give me that it isn't the time to do something you've always wanted to do, I can provide an equal number of justifications as to why it is. It is all a matter of perspective and to access the life you truly desire, you must overcome your fear of acting in the now.

If the timing is perfect, sometimes the delay comes when you wait on an individual or group to be ready to take action. Here is why I always suggest proceeding with caution when partnering with others on business ventures. You must be sure that your partner operates with the same sense of controlled urgency as you when executing a plan. If you know someone to be less than stellar in managing timeframes in their personal lives, you don't want to invite them into a scenario where their input is necessary to grow a business. If they bring some other valuable asset to the table, then construct an arrangement where you handle all time sensitive matters and can make decisions without their input.

People who work in groups at their jobs or school complain to me the most about team members who delay the completion of a project. I was burned by that several times in college and promised myself that would never happen again. When placed in a situation where I have to work in a group, I am extremely selective about who is on my team. If I have no say in the matter, I plan from the very beginning that I will be completing the entire project by myself. I don't have an expectation that the other team members will do anything to contribute. I set a timeframe to complete the tasks myself in order to meet the deadline. If someone else chips in their fair share – great! Regardless, I know at the start of the process that the project will be completed on time. I don't care if people who didn't contribute anything get credit for the work. When it's time to get the job done, I'm not wasting energy squabbling over kudos.

2 YOUR BIG OLE BUT

The single biggest determining factor to your success is you. If you've been living a life of "why me" or "why not me," it ends today. Your accomplishments as well as your failures are your own. As soon as you take responsibility for them, you can begin to make significant changes in your life, the lives of your family members and friends and humankind in general, if you so desire. There are absolutely no limitations to what you can achieve.

You may say, "Hey Nat, what about institutional racism and poverty? Are they not factors in a person's ability to achieve?" As an African American Studies and Justice & Policy Studies double major, I would absolutely agree. I believe every single individual has not only a specific genetic DNA, but also an experience "DNA." No two individuals are the same, yet there are some shared experiences certain groups may have that either benefit them or create particular difficulties based on a given situation.

People lie, but numbers do not. You can examine tons of studies conducted for the benefit of understanding trends among certain subgroups and find overrepresentation in unemployment data, incarceration rates and infant mortality figures and underrepresentation in college graduation rates, home ownership numbers and political representation. However, just because you have a particular set of identities that have real meaning for your level of access in society, it doesn't mean you must live out a prescribed life. Greek philosopher Heraclitus noted, "The only constant in life is change." This not only means systems can be changed, but we are able to change our own selves and circumstances, constantly.

The spring of 1995 I was a sophomore in high school. If a friend wanted to get in touch with me after school, he or she would have to call me on my home phone. If I weren't there, they could leave a message - with my grandma. The best-case scenario when I returned home is that my Grandma Georgie would say, "That boy called." She didn't bother finding out names or discovering the purpose of the call. "That boy" would be the only clue on which I had to go.

The trick to communicating on the phone in those days was making sure all parties were at home to chat. You'd also have to make sure no one else in the household needed the phone. If someone were out of the house or a parent or sibling had use of the phone line, the opportunity to talk fell apart.

Just for fun, I like to imagine how I would have felt if someone from 2015 hopped in a time machine and visited me in 1995 to discuss advances in communication. The conversation would go something like this, "So in 2015, most people won't even have home phones. Cellular phones will be the primary way people talk. These phones are actually small computers that operate wirelessly and can be used to take pictures and videos, hold contact information and send electronic messages instantly. These electronic messages can be text, picture and/or video messages. You will also be able to watch movies and television shows on your device."

The next sound from me would be hysterical laughter. There was absolutely nothing of which I knew in 1995 to suggest this could be remotely possible. How in the world could a small, mobile, wireless computer replace countless existing devices as well as ones yet to be invented? Regardless, 1995's impossibility is today's reality. In order for the drastic communication evolution to take place, two factors had to be at play - belief and action. Someone believed it was possible to shoot high definition videos through a cellular phone and they inspired an army of techies to take action and make it happen. Your belief combined with action can yield you similarly unbelievable results.

As a matter of fact, the only difference between you and the group that developed the first stages of GPS technology is belief. My uncle Robert, who was in the Coast Guard in addition to working many years as an engineer for the United States government was actually involved in the development of the Global Positioning System. One day it was a far-fetched idea until someone went into action and made it a tool that almost completely replaced those maps folks used to store in car glove compartments.

Belief works the other way as well. My favorite quote from Henry Ford is, "whether you think you can or you can't, you're right." Ford knew that the success or failure of any endeavor starts with the positive or negative thoughts laying dormant in your mind.

If you think you'll never amount to anything because no one in your family has amounted to anything, you are setting your course for a life filled with disappointing results. Your peak salary, physical abilities, creative contribution and impact on the world begin in your mind. The outside factors at play around you shape some components about how your journey might look, but the only person who can completely shut you out of the game is you.

Once you've made up in your mind that you want something different in your life, your *but* can be your undoing. "I want to start this new business, *but* I don't have time." "I want to improve my health, *but* there are no healthy eateries in my area." "I want to find true love, *but* I can't because I have kids." ENOUGH!

A wise person once told me, you can have excuses or results, but you can't have both. Continue to believe in your *but* and that's all of which you will be left.

Excuses are really just tools to release you from personal responsibility if you don't achieve your desired outcome. Honestly, we don't want to be embarrassed if we tell our friends we plan to lose 20 pounds, but instead gain ten. Rather than acknowledging we didn't fully commit to the process, we say something outside of our control led to the failure. "I would have been able to do it, *but* I have a slow metabolism!" I've used that one a few times, knowing full well that I had no medical data to make the claim. It just sounded much better than 'I'm on a diet of cookies and chili fries'.

In some instances, we begin setting up excuses before we even start the process. This strategy makes it easier to explain why our program didn't work out as planned. Whatever barriers we construct in our minds will appear almost on cue. When we plan to fail, failure absolutely will not fail us.

Even focusing on the fear of failure can lead us down a path to realizing that fear. Our mind doesn't distinguish empowering thoughts from destructive one. It simply moves us in the direction of the prevailing thought pattern, regardless of the level of consciousness. If you are thinking, "I don't want to fail," over and over again, your mind zips right past the other information and straight to FAIL. In order to achieve the highest level of success, we have to shift our focus.

I took the liberty of compiling a Big BUT List to demonstrate the diverse range of reasons we give for not reaching our full potential. Many of them have very real limitations to access within our society. That cannot be denied. However, this book is intended to be solution driven and not problem focused. After you review the Big BUT List, note *buts* you are actively using or have the potential to use in the future. If I missed a few of your *buts,* feel free to add them.

Big BUT List (abridged)

But I don't have enough money

But I'm not talented

But I don't have enough time

But I'm not a great communicator

But I'm not smart enough

But I don't have the right experience

But I'm not very organized

But my family/friends said I couldn't

But I have so much on my plate

But I don't know how to get started

But I didn't go to the right school

But I don't have a car

But I don't have access to public transportation

But I'm too old

But I'm too young

But I am in poor health

But I'm (insert your ethnicity)

But I'm (insert your spiritual belief)

But I'm (insert your gender)

But I'm (insert your sexuality)

But I have kids

But I don't have kids

Big BUT List (continued)

But I'm too weak

But I'm too assertive

But I didn't have a father

But I didn't have a mother

But nobody in my family has done it

But I'm not bold enough

But I am not good looking enough

But I'm too good looking to be taken seriously

But I am not tall enough

But I am too tall

But I've always done this

But I'm overweight

But I'm skinny

But I spent time in jail/prison

But my teachers said I couldn't

But I have a physical disability

But nobody doing it looks like me

But I don't have the right clothes

But I have had a troubling past

But I have an accent

But I am from another country

But I am afraid of public speaking

Big BUT List (continued)

But I'm on medication

But I need to be on medication

But I need to get my life together first

But I am single

But I'm married

But my spouse is unsupportive

But I have a bad boss

But I don't know many people

But I just moved

But I am a veteran

But I don't have any specialized training

But I am shy

But I am not good with numbers

But I am not a good writer

But I don't know how to use the computer

But I am different than everybody

But I am not unique

But I am afraid it's not going to work

But I am afraid of what I will do if it works

But I'm not educated

But I'm not a people person

But I have limited access to resources

Big BUT List (continued...AGAIN)

But I'm worried about what people will say

But I don't have a job

But my job is so taxing

But no one will give me a shot

But I have poor credit

But I don't want to ruin my good credit

But no one believes in me

But I tried before

But I'm not the right type

But what if they judge me

But no one's done this before

But I have/had a drug problem

But I was fired

But I filed for bankruptcy

But I am on public assistance

But I'm not a leader

BUT I'M SCARED

Please note that I saved the biggest *BUT* for the end. While most will not admit it, fear is the *but* of all *buts*! Typically, we use the others as scapegoats for what's really going on. We are so afraid to put ourselves out there and go for what we truly want in life. If we do that and fail, not only will the people around us lose faith in our abilities, but we will also lose faith in ourselves.

From But to Better

Today, however, is a new day. You've already made the commitment just a few pages ago to change your life and that starts with acknowledging your *buts* and moving passed them. In your *but* acknowledgement, it's okay to share your truth. My *but* acknowledgment is that research shows that as an African American woman, I am traditionally paid less than my male and Caucasian counterparts in the workforce. That's real. I am determined that although it is a real part of my story, that it is not the end of it. These factors, in addition to all the others that fall outside of my control, simply create some tension in my tale. No matter what, I am still the author. The finale is mine to design!

If that analogy was not strong enough for you, let's try another. Imagine you are a builder paid millions of dollars to construct a state of the art office complex. This is your dream building and to boot, you have been offered more money than you've ever been paid to complete the project. As a result, you put a down payment on a beautiful new home that you could not have afforded were it not for this opportunity.

Before you get started, you discover there's a problem with the site and months of additional work must be done prior to breaking ground. Next, a natural disaster delays the shipment of key equipment from overseas. Your site is fined monetarily when some workers accidentally block a street during a concrete delivery. Midway through construction, a flaw in the design is discovered. You lose several of your key personnel for a week after a food poisoning incident. Basically, everything challenging that can happen does happen.

You never once think about returning the check to the company who contracted you for the task. You never once say, "this is not going to get finished." No doubt, you're frustrated by the challenges. You might even have a few extra gray hairs or a few missing hairs as a result, but you don't say, "bad weather prevented me from achieving my goal." You push through as long as it takes until the structure is complete.

When overcoming your *buts*, you have to incorporate the same methodical and relentless pursuit of success. As soon as a *but* appears, whether real or imagined, your mission is to work around it, work through it or crush it. Stopping is never an option.

3 SELF-CENTERED VS. CENTERED SELF

One common response when people start to identify and structure a plan to eliminate *buts* is they want to attack them from the outside. The mission turns into a fight against injustice or poverty or global warming and not the biggest enemy - your *but*. Certainly those are incredibly important issues we should be dedicating time to, however, we have to create a balance that gives us the space to strengthen ourselves. When we are broken, we are limited in our capability to fight against larger global concerns. This scenario is much like what we are directed to do if oxygen levels in an airplane cabin decrease. We must secure our masks before assisting others. This very real life or death situation reminds us that we can't help anyone else until we help ourselves.

The starting point for this process begins with self-examination. You can't really know what you need until you honestly evaluate what's going on inside your heart and your head. Even though this can be a scary venture, it's well worth the effort of digging through the cobwebs and skeletons hidden inside. This is a time to really become centered, but in order to do that; you must know exactly what centered is and what it isn't.

Self-Centered

If I asked you to take some time to think of the names of a few self-centered people in your life, I'm sure you wouldn't have too much trouble. These are the folks who can eat up a whole coffee break, lunch meeting, happy hour or phone chat talking about themselves. Some of the really egregious ones don't even bother to ask you the cursory "and what about you" during the last 45 seconds of the exchange.

Before you get on your high horse, just know that this is not intended to start an attack on the self-centered. We all have our moments of thinking the world revolves around us. Most of us, however, have been trained to keep that hidden. We smile, nod and act thoroughly interested in what another person is sharing, but inside, we're making a mental grocery list. Yes, that qualifies us all, as being self-centered as we are saying in that moment, a carton of almond milk is more important than another person's share.

Don't beat yourself up. As I mentioned, this is not about being self-centered, but rather making a distinction between being self-centered and being your centered self. It is important that we all focus on our center and create time in our lives to work on perfecting our machine. Humans require constant maintenance and not just to our physical selves, but our emotional, mental and spirituals selves as well. Self-centered people aren't necessarily doing the work, but rather use the attention of others as a patch. Most often it's a scenario that the more people focus on them, the less they have to truly focus on themselves.

Centered Self

Being centered means that you have the best opportunity to help others as opposed to those who are chronically self-centered and quite simply just shining a spotlight on their own brokenness. When you're centered, you don't need anyone to know all your details of greatness. Your focus is much more balanced and you can support your loved ones from a place of genuine kindness, with no expectation of acknowledgement. You know who you are. You don't need others to toot your horn and alert the village of your arrival.

Getting to your centered self is not easy. This journey begins with you acknowledging that on some level, you don't have it together. Go into a brief moment of introspection. Think about why you wanted to read this book in the first place. You will likely find an answer there. (If you are my mom, don't worry; you are perfect and I know you're only reading this to support me. Thanks!)

Whether your list of items to work on is one, two or ten tweaks long, begin with the most important adjustment and work your way down. Throughout the next few chapters, I will share some tips on how to work through the list, but for now just make sure you have it.

Confessions of a Recovering Self-Centered Person

In 2002, I was an ambitious graduate student at Cornell University, finishing up the coursework for my master's degree while zeroing in on a thesis topic. I had been a taskmaster as it related to ticking things off of my life checklist. I graduated from an outstanding undergraduate liberal arts school, Guilford College and had gotten into several top graduate programs in the country before choosing to attend Cornell. I was studying something I loved, in spite of the confused gazes of relatives and older friends. Some wondered why as an African American, I'd be studying African American Studies at all. Shouldn't I just know everything already? For me, this was like saying, because we are human, we need not study anatomy. Everyone inherently knows the complete functionality of his or her thyroid.

Anyway, I digress. I was completely content and feeling like Midas touching every opportunity and turning it gold. However, there was one rather looming item staring back at me from my list - husband. You see, while my Grandma Nancy never believed there was such a thing as African American Studies, she was willing to go along with the program. In her eyes there were only four true professional options - doctor, lawyer, teacher and business owner. No matter what I told her I was going to do with a master's in African American Studies, it wasn't going to fit into one of those jobs. After our discussions, she'd give a look, but wait until I was gone to express her true feelings on the matter. Though when it came to relationships, grandma wanted, nay, needed to know, there was some movement toward a marriage.

Everything was lined up in my life, but that, until I encountered another ambitious Cornellian also in the market for a partner. Was there love? Absolutely. However, the catch was that at that moment we were both operating from self-centered positions. We were both intent on finding a spouse and low and behold, a match was made. Had we been operating from a centered place, I am certain we would have taken a little more time to let the dust settle on the relationship before racing down the aisle.

There was, in our world, no time to hesitate. Four months after our first date, we began planning our wedding and before the ink was dry on my degree, we were snorkeling on our Jamaican honeymoon. We both had accomplished a great thing uniting our Ivy League super forces, but what we didn't expect was the war of wills that would ensue. This, my friends, is the first thing that happens when you operate from a self-centered place instead of a centered place.

Centered people never have to prove themselves or bend others to their will. They know exactly who they are and feel confident advocating for themselves. Self-centered people actually lack confidence. No matter how they portray themselves, there is a constant and gnawing need to control the external instead of addressing the internal deficit.

We spent the first few months battling for position in a condo so small, we could see or hear each other regardless of where the other person was unless one of us was in the bathroom. I reminded him constantly of my sacrifice relocating to the other side of the country to accommodate his professional ambitions and he reminded me of how he was working two jobs to keep us financially afloat. Not many knew it, but there were a few times that I began to think about how I could justify keeping our beautiful bath towels if an abrupt end came to our very short marriage.

Instead of giving up, we gave in to living the American dream. We lived and worked in several places across the country. We made friends. We made lots of business moves. And lastly, we made it a point to continue the same battle of who sacrificed the most for years, until we finally dedicated ourselves to being friends instead of spouses. It wasn't until after we'd moved on with our respective romantic lives that I figured out the idea of centered self vs. self-centered.

If you think you might be operating from a self-centered place or if you know with absolute certainty that you are, please proceed with caution when entering into a relationship. This is not to suggest you must be completely centered when you start dating, but you have to know that the difference in mindset can be very drastic. You will behave and make decisions in a totally different way depending on where you are.

Centered People	Self-Centered People
Don't need to prove a point.	Feel compelled to prove their point.
Listen empathetically.	Listen defensively.
Appreciate input.	Desire praise.
Share willingly.	Share strategically.
Know mistakes are human nature.	Know that mistakes can be exploited.

Just because you've gotten yourself to a centered place once, doesn't mean it will always last. Being centered is very similar to being in marathon condition. You will not fair well entering a 26K if your most well defined muscle is in the finger you use to change the channels of your remote control. Likewise, if you are not constantly building up your emotional, mental and spiritual self with positive information, you can easily slip back down the rabbit hole of a self-centered life.

4 GET OVER YOU THEN GET INTO YOU

In my first major transition from being self-centered to becoming my centered self, I had to get over myself, then get into myself. I know that seems a bit weird, but I promise it will all make sense momentarily.

The first step of course, was to get over myself. I was a single woman again, living in New York City. It was the perfect place to get over myself. For those of you who have experienced life in New York, even if for a quick vacation, you know that to survive there, you must have your wits about you. I didn't have the time or financial resources to wallow, so immediately, I had to create a new life and identity for myself.

At the point when the break up was absolutely final, I moved out of our beautiful Manhattan condo to a three bedroom apartment shared with two other women in Sunnyside, Queens. I loaded all my stuff in the small bedroom adjacent to the living room and started anew. Before I could get unpacked, my friend Misha, had us heading to the Mets season opener at Citifield. If I'd had my way, I would have taken the afternoon to cry a bit having left some amazing furniture, wedding mementos, an apartment a block from Central Park, but most importantly the longest and most significant relationship of my adult life. Instead, I was eating hot dogs and nachos in some pretty awesome seats at the game.

I came back to my room and still didn't cry. I was too tired. The next few days contained more of the same. My calendar was packed with activities and auditions for acting roles. When I finally had time to reflect, I reminded myself that I was not a victim in this situation. I made choices that impacted the status of our relationship. There were occasions where I didn't speak up when I felt hurt. Other times, I didn't communicate appropriately when I did feel compelled to share. Both of our fingerprints were on the divorce, just as both of them were on the marriage.

Victim Mentality

The self-centered victim mentality had prevented me from being solution oriented in my marriage. Those of us, who chronically assume that role, can be the most self-centered. As victims, life is happening to us and not because of us. We believe that somehow, the universe is conspiring against us. To remain in the comfort of this position, we must constantly remind everyone around us of our struggle.

I am in no way attacking people who are facing hardships. Rather, I am suggesting a victimhood mentality is dangerously self-centered and sometimes difficult to overcome. In the moments where I was completely immersed in my own problems, I felt I deserved my victim status and no one could tell me my suffering wasn't worth lamenting at every opportunity.

The divorce left me with no one to blame for anything. I was totally in charge of my existence as a single person. Over time, I realized through my personal development journey that I was in charge when I was married as well. I had simply chosen to bundle the things I didn't like about the relationship and myself as symptoms of the marriage. One example is for years I believed my professional career was stunted because we moved so often for his work. The truth is, I am and have always been meant to be my own boss. I learned invaluable lessons from employers across the country on how to effectively run my own businesses. Perhaps if I had been in one location for an extended period of time, I would not have tapped into my entrepreneurial side so quickly.

If you have some blame lingering in your heart for a former lover, business partner, co-worker, friend, relative, etc, do yourself a favor and let go of it immediately. Holding on keeps you in a position of victimhood and you cannot progress if you never believe you have control over your life to do so.

Success Projectors

The victim mentality is not the only way self-centeredness is manifested. Plenty of people move through life as *success projectors*. *Success projectors* are the folks you know who claim to always have something amazing going on. They are a big deal everywhere, all the time. They are name-droppers who move and shake all over the globe. *Success projectors* also know a bit about everything. If you bring up a topic, they either have intimate knowledge of it or have people close to them who are highly involved.

There is nothing wrong with being positive and success oriented. I am a big proponent of focusing conversations and thoughts on winning as opposed to losing. I only post positive information on my social media regarding my projects and personal affairs. I avoid spending a tremendous amount of time communicating about hardship and loss, because most often, I am using my energy to build instead of continually discussing what is broken.

The difference between people who are success oriented and those who are *success projectors* is buried beneath the surface. Underneath it all, success oriented people not only want success for themselves, but for those around them. *Success projectors* want success, but most importantly, they want you to know about it.

My cousin, Nancy, is one of the most successful people I know. She graduated from Harvard, won the Miss Virginia pageant, is a New York Times Best Selling author and is currently an amazing host on HuffPost Live. She's a great mom, wife, daughter, sister, aunt and friend and I've never once heard her toot her own horn. Sometimes, I find out a great event has happened in her life through her brother Sammy's social media posts. This is one of the things I love most about her. Anytime we have the opportunity to chat on the phone, she cares more about finding out what I'm doing and providing words of encouragement. Nancy makes no mention of the celebrities she's interviewed that week. I only know from frequenting the HuffPost Live site.

By all means, it is not a negative thing to share the wonderful events taking place in your life. Good stories need to be shared and celebrated. Success oriented people are adept at sharing accomplishments without the "rub your nose in it" factor. *Success projectors* like it when you know they are doing so much more (even when they're not), while success oriented people would rather we all do more together.

Getting Over You

It doesn't matter if you have a victim mentality or if you're stuck in the cycle of a *success projector*, you can begin today to move into a more productive place. Start your transition with a little self-talk. Locate a mirror. Stare at your reflection for a few minutes then begin reading the script that applies to you.

Victim mentality transition self-talk: (Insert your name), for years I've allowed myself to be beaten down by the world. I've let everybody and their momma know about every hardship I've ever had. My conversation and my thoughts have been a reflection of everything I don't want in life. Today, however, is a new day. Today, I will focus my mind on the great things I have and the wonderful things that I want. When someone asks me how I'm doing, I will pause to think about all the things for which I am grateful. No matter how challenging the day is I will always have a spirit of gratitude and a zest for life.

Success projector transition self-talk: (Insert your name), for years I've presented a façade of having it all together. I've intentionally misrepresented my circumstances in an effort to make others feel like I'm doing better than my peers. I know deep down inside that this is because I feel like I should be doing better than I really am. Today, however, is a new day. Today, I will focus my mind on the great things I have and the wonderful things that I want. When someone ask me how I'm doing, I will pause to think about all the things for which I am grateful. No matter how deep the urge to be impressive, I will instead be honest. My life is wonderful as it is, without having to hide behind embellishments.

General positive self-talk: (Insert name), for years I have not lived my absolute best life. I've allowed obstacles both internal and external to keep me from reaching my full potential. Regardless from whence they came, I allowed them to stunt my growth. Today, however, is a new day. Today, I will focus my mind on the great things I have and the wonderful things that I want. No matter what the day brings me, I will have an attitude of gratitude.

Getting Into You

After your self-talk time is done, continue looking in the mirror for a few more minutes. Smile at yourself. Wink at yourself. Laugh at yourself. You are smart, beautiful, loving, compassionate and fearless. Once you are over the toxic you, it's time to get into the amazing you. He or she is looking back at you in the mirror and is 100% equipped to create the most incredible life imaginable. You just need to get to know exactly with whom you're dealing.

Typically the first few weeks/months of dating a new person is dedicated to finding out all the details of his/her life. Favorite colors, favorite movies, favorite vacations spots and favorite hobbies are, in that moment, the critical pieces of information that can make or break any young relationship. If you are a die-hard Sci-Fi fan and your new boo thinks Trekkies are people who like hiking, your relationship could potentially be doomed.

While the exploration does move beyond the topic of favorites, these initial connections (or lack thereof) can determine whether or not a relationship will persist. The funny thing is we invest a lot of time in discovering all the nuances of a potential partner and hardly know anything about ourselves. It's easy for me to share that *Coming to America* is one of my favorite movies, but it takes a bit more effort to explore why. The "why" of the response is rarely ever investigated and that truly is where the deeper self-understanding is found.

I was 9 years old when *Coming to America* was released in theaters. I lobbied for weeks to see the movie, but my mom was firm that I was too young. She was also quite displeased that my father had even allowed me to become such a huge Eddie Murphy fan. My dad and I literally watched *Beverly Hills Cop* every single weekend I visited him. We knew every line and had the signature Eddie Murphy laugh down to a science. When the advertisements for *Coming to America* came out, I absolutely had to see it. I made outrageous, unachievable promises about the chores I would complete and the grades I would receive if I were allowed to go see it with my dad.

Eventually, my mom gave in and granted us permission to go. Dad and I squeezed into a row of the crowded theater after the movie had already started. It didn't matter that we were late. I was in heaven. I was at the new Eddie Murphy movie with my buddy - nothing was better.

Beyond the fact that Eddie Murphy is a comedic genius and *Coming to America* is totally hilarious, the reason I will always love the movie is because of the experience with my dad. And while you may think that this is hardly an important self-discovery, I want you to know that every major life decision, personality quirk, career interest and even personal style is built on small pieces of information like this.

Is it a coincidence that I have a passion for screen writing and that comedy is my favorite genre to write? Nope. We are constructed like magnificent paintings. It is impossible for a beautiful piece to come together without the tiny speckles of paint. While one speckle does not tell the whole story, it can have significant meaning when placed into the context of the others.

As you ask yourself questions, no matter how trivial they may seem, dig deep within to identify a response that gives you more than just the answer, but also leads you to a new level of understanding. You can also feel free to work this exploration plan from the other direction. Ask yourself a question like, "Why am I passionate about children's rights?" After you discover the answer, ask "why?" for that. This will start to seem like the same questioning technique children utilize, because it is.

A child can drive you crazy with a long string of "whys." Even though it is maddening, you know it's because they haven't yet had enough life experiences to understand the meaning of words and situations. Eventually, most of us shut off the line of questions with "because I said so" or "just because."

What we don't realize is that we use the same strategy during our own moments of self-discovery. It can be taxing to keep going and the easy way out is to think "just because."

No matter how challenging it gets, commit to the process. I guarantee you will discover information of far greater significance than the title of your favorite movie. Through this exploration you can identify your triggers and can begin to diffuse them. You finally know why you are so bothered when you see someone not wearing a seat belt, because you remember banging your head against the back of the seat when you were younger while not wearing one. The pain faded eventually and the memory became distant, but you were impacted forever by the experience.

The hundreds of "whys" you uncover can change your life and perspective. However, this is not an exercise in dwelling on the past, but instead a time to acknowledge every tree has a root. There is nothing about your life that just appeared from thin air. Everything you are and everything you believe came from an experience or a genetic predisposition. The reason for all reactions and responses is buried deep within. Your task is to find it, acknowledge it and make adjustments to your actions if these "roots" prove to be harmful in your everyday life.

It goes without saying, sometimes when we begin to unearth challenging experiences, we might need help processing them. Do not feel the least bit ashamed if you need to find assistance. It's so much better to ask for help and not ultimately need it than to not ask and find yourself in the throws of a mental, emotional or spiritual health crisis. Moreover, I am not here to recommend a particular type of assistance. Your beliefs, personal history and social comfort make certain programs or processes work for you while others won't. Put the effort into finding a process or person who can help you rather than focusing on all the things you believe are ineffective.

One easy technique for getting into you is to fully experience life. When you feel a shift in emotions during the day, make a note of when it happened and what was going on at the time. If you don't have time to think through what triggered the change in emotions right away, then set aside a moment for reflection at the end of the day. Use your notes to remember the instances where your emotions shifted. Do your best to trace back the feeling. Sometimes, you won't be able to find the root right away. Go as far as you can, then commit to working on the process later when you have more time. If you start to feel overwhelmed, stop and plug into a support system before continuing.

Here are a few questions you can ask yourself to begin your exploration. If you are comfortable sharing this experience with loved ones, it could be a great opportunity to have a support person present during your discovery process. Additionally, they can be helpful in filling in some information you might not remember. Parents and siblings can assist you in recalling events that may be foggy in your mind. Remember, though, that this is about your journey, not theirs. It is important to know why these details are significant for you, not for them.

Self-Check

1. How did I end up in my current profession? What was the path to being in this position?

2. What do I love about my life? What would I like to change?

3. What pivotal moments in my life shaped the person I've become? Why do these moments stand out? What life decisions did I make as a result of these events?

4. What do I hope to accomplish in the next month, next year and next five years? How did I arrive at these goals? How are they different from goals I had last month, last year and five years ago?

5. Have my dreams and goals changed because of positive life experiences or negative ones? What specifically has altered my path?

6. What are the dominant emotions that I experience throughout the day? What events typically trigger these emotions?

7. What am I known for amongst my friends, family and colleagues? For what would I like to be known?

8. If I could live anywhere in the world, where would it be? Why do I want to live there? If I am not in my dream location now, why is that?

9. What are the things in life I want, but do not currently have? What is keeping me from having them?

10. What are my favorite books, movies, plays, vacation spots, stores, etc? Why do I love them?

Bookmark this page as you might not be able to finish answering all of the questions in one sitting. The deeper you dig into your responses, the more time it is likely to take. It's perfectly okay to read the entire book and still not be finished with this self-check. Your goal should be answering the questions honestly and thoroughly.

5 MISSION AND MOVEMENTS

Real change happens when you take real action. There's no way around that simple fact. For better or worse, we have become a society of politicians. We use dinner parties, water cooler chats and social media posts to profess our ideals. We share advertisements in the form of links to news articles and inspirational quotes to get the message we believe is important out to the people.

Although I am terribly bothered by the mudslinging and fact manipulation associated with the political campaign process, I am very much involved in personal campaigning on social media. I post information that reflects my belief system and I am excited when friends and family "vote for" aka like what I've shared. It feels good to know you are in the company of other like-minded people as a member of the "Entrepreneur for Life" party or the "Success Quotes Are The Best" party. Hopefully one of these parties will have some representation in the next general election.

Creating social groups constructed around a similar belief system is not a new concept. Every fraternity/sorority, faith based organization and social club is set up to recruit and corral members as well as promote the group's mission.

There is nothing inherently wrong with the model. The problematic concern arises when the espoused beliefs of the collective is disconnected from the actual actions of the group. To put it plainly, the mouth is saying one thing, but the body is actually doing another.

In January 2004, I moved to Detroit, Michigan. I was tremendously excited to connect with the people and culture of Motown. The experience did not disappoint, but admittedly it was a bittersweet year and a half. At that time, you could drive through particular neighborhoods where at the start of the block there was a beautifully maintained house, which was next to a vacant lot, which was next to a burned out house, which was next to a house in disarray, which was next to a beautifully maintained house. The economic hardship the community faced was painfully apparent.

This tore at my heartstrings as I came to know and love so many native Detroiters. One morning, while in route to a church we'd never been to, we drove through an entire area that was once a bustling commercial district. We passed rows and rows of boarded up stores and businesses. For a moment, it felt like being in an area that had been completely deserted. Several blocks later, however, we arrived at our destination - a huge church.

The parking ministry guided us to a parking spot. The members of the usher board helped us find a seat. The choir sang like angels. The experience was amazing and awful at the same time. I couldn't shake the image of the abandoned zombie land we drove through to get there. I prayed that very soon there would be an announcement about an initiative to revitalize the community. I had only been in Detroit for a week and a half, but was ready to commit time and financial resources to what every church espouses as their mission - to help the least of these. Clearly, there were real people who owned and/or worked in those businesses that were in need of opportunities and I didn't imagine all of them had left the neighborhood.

I sat on the edge of my seat - waiting. I looked around the auditorium knowing that everyone there had been impacted by the fledgling economy to some degree. I wanted church to be over so we could do something together to re-build. My stomach bubbled with anticipation. I knew something had to be going on here and to my chagrin, there was. Partway through the service, the dreaded announcements began about the new building fund. My heart sank. Millions of dollars were being raised to construct a new state of the art facility amidst the ruins of a dynamic community.

This was a moment where I wished I did not have home training. I not only wanted to storm out, but I also wanted to give a nice, loud, crazy lady rant as I left. The message would have been sound, but the curse words imbedded within would have definitely sent it over the top.

Before church folks start casting me into the lake of fire for talking about building funds, please note that I have nothing against creating beautiful sanctuaries for worship. Groups can and should invest in facilities that meet their needs. However, if your primary purpose is service, but the vast financial and human resources of your powerful group is directed almost wholly into building a beautiful facility in a depressed neighborhood - I'm not with it!

I'm certain someone, somewhere said, "This new edifice will be a place the neighborhood can be proud of." I say, "hooey!" Detroiters take pride in producing. If you throw a rock in any direction on a street in Detroit, at least two hard workers will be there to catch it and fashion it into a tool. So, don't tell me that the people want a shiny new building and not entrepreneurial classes or small business grants. In the midst of struggle, it's not the time to erect some stone symbol of "spiritual prosperity" in the name of ministers securing bragging rights as to who has the largest steeple.

We left that Sunday and found what we were truly looking for, a church that responded to the needs of the community. It was located in the heart of the city and had a leadership team focused on job creation, support for the elderly and homeless as well as providing educational opportunities for young people. To be fair, this church had a building fund as well. It was used in large part, to make improvements to the existing facility. The key mission of this group was not to build buildings, but to build people.

Mission and Movements Out of Alignment

Now what in the world does my church philosophy have to do with you? Everything. My tale of two churches is about your mission and your movements being in alignment. To the best of your ability, the things you say and do should match. Is perfection an option? Not if you are human. However, don't let your human tendency to make mistakes create for you an excuse to say whatever you like and do the opposite.

One of my favorite sketch comedy shows of all-time is *In Living Color*. Miss Benita Butrell was a character featured on several episodes. Her big claim to fame was she wasn't one to gossip, but the whole skit consisted of her gossiping. While Kim Wayans was absolutely hilarious in this role, the element that made it over the top funny for me was that it was real. I could relate to Miss Benita's character because I knew so many people like her. At the core, these people weren't bad or malicious; it was just that their mission and their movements were not in alignment.

How does this happen? Don Miguel Ruiz does an outstanding job of explaining this in his book, *The Four Agreements*. Essentially, he shares that we are taught the rules of our society from the first moments we are outside the womb. The people around us teach us the "right" way to be through punishments and rewards.

Even when behaviors aren't natural to who we are at our core, we hide our true selves in order to avoid punishments and secure rewards. We learn from our community what is valued and we try to fit as best as possible into the accepted mold.

So much conflict arises in our spirits as we attempt to manage all of the outside messages and expectations. We become actors presenting different facades to different people in order to be accepted. It doesn't take much of an imagination to see how playing multiple roles at any given time can be highly problematic. Tyler Perry may be adept at juggling these varied characters on screen, but this is not a healthy arrangement in the real world.

For many years I worked in the higher education field and at a certain point, social media became a common communication tool. I attended countless workshops and seminars on how to structure an appropriate professional profile or the dos and don'ts of interacting with students on social media. As the power of these websites and applications grew, so did the policies around how we could manage them. Colleges strictly enforced rules around posting information pertaining to certain work experiences. Administrators sometimes scrutinized pictures and videos posted. The result was that many of my colleagues created separate work and personal profiles.

While I neither agree nor disagree with the creation of a personal and a professional profile, it absolutely underscores my point regarding the ease with which we can become completely disjointed. The funny, shoe loving, practical joking Natalie that wears monkey slippers around the house is the same Natalie who delivers professional presentations in front of thousands. Is it impossible for me to be silly and taken seriously at the same time?

As much as there is a struggle to juggle multiple personas for the sake of pleasing others, it seems nearly impossible to present your whole self to everyone.

The last thing you want in life is to present the true you and for that to be rejected because it doesn't fit the mold. So much about our culture embraces at minimum a certain level of duality. Take for example the following phrases:

1. Don't mix business and personal affairs

2. Work/life balance

3. A lady in the streets, but a freak in the bed

Every phrase seems logical within the structure of our societal/cultural norms, but when you really break each one down, it starts to feel supremely confusing. The two ways of being are in conflict, but the expectation is a person will effectively be able to manage both. Although number 3 is a very real example, if you didn't get a chuckle out of seeing it there, you're missing a great comedy pit stop on the journey.

In a previous chapter, I mentioned every tree has a root. The persona confusion we grapple with from our first days onward is the root cause of the mixed messages we send into the world when we become fully grown. As I noted before, it's not always intentional, however, when we develop an awareness about this issue, we must take the steps to re-align.

If you're starting to question whether your espoused beliefs and actions are in alignment, great! I put together a short self-check to help you uncover some answers. If you feel like you are in perfect alignment, definitely go through the self-check. To write this book, I have gone through several years of concentrated personal development and I am certain that I am still not in 100% alignment. The tiny percent of the population who are closest to the goal of 100% alignment would most likely never claim it. They are so focused on constantly improving themselves; they can identify microscopic flaws in the execution of their personal philosophy.

Self-Check: True or False

1. There are things I do in some areas of my life that I wouldn't want certain people to know.

2. I often give advice contrary to what I personally carry out in my own life.

3. I have recently spoken negatively about someone in a conversation, but would be hurt if those negative descriptions were shared about me.

4. I am currently holding a grudge against someone, but believe that any mistakes I have made in the past should be forgiven.

5. I feel like it's necessary to tell people what they need to hear even if it isn't the whole truth, but I, myself, hate being misled.

6. I present a lifestyle in person and on social media that is not in line with my current financial situation.

7. I embellish my achievements and/or credentials on my resume to make myself more impressive to a potential employer, but would be frustrated if the salary or job requirements for a position were posted inaccurately.

8. If my friends knew who I really am, I don't think they'd like me.

9. I often agree with people to avoid conflict.

10. I can think of an instance in the past few days where I've lied to receive a reward or to avoid a punishment.

The more "true" responses you have from the self-check, the more work you will need to do to align your mission and your movements. I intentionally included some checkpoints to make you think about what you believe is acceptable to give versus what you believe is acceptable to receive. You can call it a forced A-Ha moment.

This may be a great time to take a short break from the book to reflect, but not long enough for you to forget about it and never finish it. To get everything you need out of this process, you genuinely have to examine who you are, what is important to you and what is holding you back from being one strong person as opposed to ten fragile personas. Sometimes I power through a book with more excitement about finishing it than absorbing all of the information. It's like I imagine there is some reward for having a high book completion rate.

Let me assure you, no one is keeping score here, but you. Take the time you need to get all you can out of the process. If you are someone who just can't recover when you feel like reading momentum is lost, bookmark all of the pages that require additional work and commit to returning.

Finally, as you discover and re-discover yourself, remember to operate with some flexibility. You are allowed to change your mission, just remember to update your movements when that change takes place.

6 JOY THIEVES

A common setback many people have when they are really starting to create positive change in their lives comes from those with whom they associate. Friends, family and acquaintances who are Negative Nellies can completely derail the process. Warning: do not take this as an opportunity to blame those around you for your lack of improvement. With the exception of family and some co-workers, you chose the negative folks in your life. Just as easily as you connected with them, you can disconnect from them. As for the negative people you absolutely cannot cut out of your life, you can better manage their affect on you. This process can begin by reducing the time you spend with them.

I commonly call the negative people in my life, *joy thieves*. I use this term for a couple of reasons. The first is that whether intentional or not, they can swipe joy, happiness, positivity and fun from a situation or conversation. The second reason is, while they have the full capability to be a thief, it does not mean they are always successful. We determine whether or not a *joy thief* is able to scurry off with our good feelings. We must at all times protect our valuables. I try to always lock up my positive energy just like I'd lock up handful of flawless diamonds.

How do you know if someone is a *joy thief*? Start with the names that popped into your head when you read the title of the chapter. It isn't hard to know who brings your mood down when you speak to them on the phone or meet them in person. They are always sick, always have a complaint, always gossiping about other people and typically are unsupportive of any activities/changes in your life that don't include them.

Joy thieves reading this will most likely have a long list of people they believe are *joy thieves* and scoff at the idea that they are, in fact, at the top of several other people's list. Hopefully, this self-check will help some *joy thieves* identify themselves and begin making the necessary adjustments to change.

FYI, for the sake of transparency, please note that I really struggle with number 5 and have improved greatly, but still am a work in progress for number 7 and number 10. The reason I am being honest about my challenges is because I want you to have the courage to be honest about yours. We can't be our best selves if we aren't truthful about our reality.

Self-Check: True or False

1. I frequently find myself frustrated or angry as a result of other people's actions and feel compelled to comment.

2. When something negative happens to me, I will talk about it with anyone who will listen.

3. I am not on speaking terms with several friends or family members who have wronged me.

4. In conversations about my health, I typically focus on poor health over wellness.

5. I enjoy listening to and/or sharing juicy gossip.

6. People have commented on my negativity or frequent complaints in the past.

7. I sometimes find joy when someone who has wronged me is experiencing a hardship. I feel like they are getting their just due.

8. People are often against me.

9. Most people can't deal with my "keep it real" attitude.

10. I rarely apologize after an argument and if I do, I'll never apologize first.

The more "true" responses you had, the more likely you are a *joy thief*. If you were either huffy after reading the self-check or felt like it had no grounds as an assessment, you are likely a *joy thief*. Sincerely, this is not designed to make you feel bad, it's to help you understand that the source of negativity in your life is you. This can be an amazing turning point for you and your family if you allow it. Review the self-check again if you had negative feelings toward it, because therein lies a sign that the term *joy thief* could apply to you.

Protecting Yourself Against Theft

As I mentioned earlier, the best way to protect your joy from thieves is to disassociate yourself from people who are consistently negative. You may feel like this is a cold move, but you're really not doing them any favors by sticking around. You are essentially co-signing on their negative attitude by being party to it. Additionally, you may be thought of as a *joy thief* by association if you are seen frequently hanging out with a known offender.

If you identify most of the people in your life as *joy thieves*, then you are probably a *joy thief* in denial. Remember in most cases, like connects with like. You don't regularly see millionaires with homeless people in their close circle of friends. It's not because they have completely opposite interests. However, their lives and daily activities are so drastically different, there really is no space for genuine long-term connections.

If your day-to-day activities put you in the position to spend most of your time with *joy thieves*, then you are in a "birds of a feather flock together" scenario and you're going to have to make some definitive changes to disconnect from the group.

Here are some quick tips you can use to protect yourself against joy theft:

1. Tip the balance by spending more time with people who are positive.

2. Join groups or organizations whose mission and movements are based on positive principles.

3. Read and/or listen to inspirational books.

4. Become more service oriented.

5. Discover what makes you unique and special, then give thanks for it every day.

6. Make gratitude lists.

7. Smile more.

8. Make a graceful exit when a *joy thief* puts his/her hand in your good feelings treasure chest.

9. Incorporate activities into your day that positively feed your body, mind and spirit.

10. Love everyone - *joy thief* or not. Whether or not we want to admit it, at some point, we've all been *joy thieves* - even if for a few short minutes while airing workplace grievances at the water cooler.

Joy Gifter

Thank goodness for *joy gifters*. They are people who brighten a room when they enter. Typically, they have something positive to say about everything and everyone. If it's a sunny day, they're happy. If it's a rainy day, they're happy. They can step in dog poop and claim it's good luck.

If you are on a *joy gifter's* social media page, you will only find inspirational quotes. They are not into posting about every disaster, crime story or personal tale of woe. They are also not engaged in passive aggressive social media beefs. You know the posts that read, "People are out here trying to test me," or "I can't stand people who think they're better than the other people in the office." *Joy gifters* don't participate in that foolery because if they have a concern that needs to be addressed with another person, they approach them directly and tactfully.

My Aunt Kate is an amazing *joy gifter*. Recently, I called her to wish her a happy birthday. 95% of the conversation, however, was her speaking positive things into my life. For everything I told her that was going on with me, she had an encouraging response. I mentioned I was writing a book. She rolled right into how I was always such a good writer. I talked about some of my recent travel adventures. She commented how excited she was for me. I told her I left my job to pursue my passion. She couldn't have been more pleased that I took such a bold step.

When we got off the phone, I felt like there was nothing in the universe I couldn't do. I wanted to go out and share my happiness with others. That's what *joy gifters* do! They inspire people to think and move beyond their present circumstances. They sincerely hope you lead a marvelous life and their impact is far more powerful than a *joy thief*.

Making the Shift

Anyone can be a *joy gifter*. It doesn't matter how long you have been a *joy thief*, you can always make the change. If you consider yourself to be neither a thief nor a gifter, you too, can benefit from these tips if you really desire to inspire and uplift the people around you.

Think before you speak. If a complaint comes to mind when you are in conversation with someone either eliminate it or re-frame it to be solution oriented instead of problem focused. Ask someone who has had the courage to give you constructive feedback in the past to let you know when you are on complaint overload just in case you have become mentally numb to your own negativity.

Avoid telling everyone about all your little nicks and scrapes. Most of us have allergies or achy joints from time to time, which shouldn't be a part of our identity when in conversation. This is not to say you should hide serious illnesses from relatives. Designate someone who can actually be of some assistance as your health accountability buddy so you have some real support when you need it. Otherwise, your neighbor's cousin need not know about your runny nose.

Stop gossiping! When negative words seep out of your lips, think of it like air pollution and joy as our precious ozone layer. You are essentially killing this critical protective barrier every time you let gossip out. Help friends make the shift too by gently changing the topic when gossip comes up or kindly cutting the conversation short. Ease out of these situations as opposed to being snippy. As a *joy gifter*, you want your interactions to be as positive as possible, so try not to pounce on someone who is still a work in progress.

Be genuinely encouraging. There are so many uplifting messages or compliments you can share with the people you encounter. You need to come from a place of honesty though, because fake encouragement is sometimes worse than no encouragement at all.

For example, if you meet a friend for lunch that is physically disheveled and she says, "I'm a mess right now." Don't respond, "no way, you look great," when you know deep in your heart that she looks frazzled. Instead of bending the truth, come up with a supportive response that is reflective of your relationship. I would probably say something like, "Honey, I've been there and it's nothing that a little shopping therapy won't cure." You have to find the words that are genuine for you though.

Great Receivers

Don't let the old saying, "tis better to give than to receive" fool you into thinking that receiving gifts is a bad thing. It's actually really amazing. Most importantly, the cycle of giving is dependent on people being receivers. The giving machine would come to a complete halt if there were no receivers available to accept its gifts. T. Harv Eker, author of *Secrets of the Millionaire Mind* even dedicates a section of his book to receiving. He asserts that when you refuse to receive, you are actually robbing the giver of the great feeling of giving.

Being a great receiver, means you not only graciously receive gifts and compliments, but also feedback and lessons. Great receivers see every moment in every day as a potential learning opportunity. Instead of moving through the day like zombies, dragging from one appointment to another, they are attentive to their surroundings. Incredible insights and inspiration could be around any corner.

Several years ago, while working as a Residence Hall Director at Stony Brook University, I encountered two great receivers. They also happened to be the most strong-willed, opinionated and ambitious young women I met in my time working with students. They were both born and raised in Connecticut in households that couldn't have been more different.

In their minds, their only commonality was their home state and their position as Resident Assistants in our building.

That year, I was so proud of the eclectic mix of personalities represented on our staff. Raj was the international student known for helping 24/7 and in some cases even over-helping. Jessika was the comedic spokesperson of the group and often could be heard on the first floor, even if she were spreading cheer on the third. Arthur aka Teddy was the RA most likely to break up tension with humor and hugs. Laraib was the perfectionist with impeccable notes on every meeting and training. Then there were the two warriors from Conn - Emma and Mary-Elizabeth.

While these two ladies had a genuine passion for helping students. Their execution styles were quite different. Mary-Elizabeth had a more reserved, traditional way of supporting. Emma, however, was anything but traditional. They bumped heads almost immediately. One staff meeting, they had a massive showdown. Tempers flared, words were exchanged and a cloud of awkwardness fell over the entire room. We were all stunned. Teddy couldn't stop it with a hug. Raj couldn't help them figure it out. Laraib had nothing in her notes to resolve the problem and Jessika for the first time, was completely silent.

I held a private meeting with them afterward and shed some light on the real problem. It wasn't a matter of difference that caused the feud, but a matter of similarity. I gave them a firm yet supportive pep talk where I noted their great similarities and my admiration for those shared traits. Even though they were furious with each other, they listened. They were open to the possibility that I could be right. There was no evidence to prove it, but because they were great receivers, they began to search for the lesson embedded within the mess. After I shared my final thoughts, I left them to figure out how they would use their super powers for good rather than evil.

From that day forward, they embarked upon a journey to get to know each other better and build a partnership based on their shared passions. Emma was on the executive team of the Center for Womyn's Concerns on campus and as their relationship continued to develop, Mary-Elizabeth became involved with the group. Today, Mary-Elizabeth is the advisor of the CWC and her innovative programming has taken the organization to new levels.

This is a fantastic example of how several gifts were born out of conflict. Emma and Mary-Elizabeth discovered an unexpected friendship and the CWC and campus as a whole benefited from their new alliance. When Emma, Mary-Elizabeth and I reflect on that moment, they give me a lot of credit for helping them see the light. I always respond that I enjoy being right, but in all honesty; I was the least important piece of the puzzle. I've facilitated countless mediations between students and colleagues that resulted in an "agree to disagree" outcome. Lessons were certainly learned, but my young protégés from Connecticut demonstrated a higher level of investment in finding a gift. Years later, that gift is still giving.

7 THERE'S A BLESSING IN THE STORM

In the grand scheme of things, Emma and Mary-Elizabeth's battle was pretty insignificant. Everyday, people all over the globe are dealing with some overwhelming circumstances. In my time of success coaching college students, I've sat with victims of sexual assault, young people who are contemplating suicide and co-eds who just learned of a parent's death.

I am happy to report that human resilience is a force to be reckoned with. Not long ago, I worked with a young woman who admitted she was suicidal. She spent several days in the hospital getting the medication and counseling services she needed to feel balanced again. Even though she missed some classes as a result of her hospitalization, she still managed to make the Dean's List. She told me that if she hadn't gotten the help, she would've probably dropped out of school or worse due to her depression. For her, the hospital stay was a tremendous blessing.

Growing up in a southern Baptist church, I often heard the saying, "there's a blessing in the storm." I had no clue what that meant as a child. I thought of things very literally and would look outside during a thunderstorm wondering where the blessing was. I wasn't even sure what a blessing looked like. It sounded like a great name for a pony, so perhaps I'd see one and my parents would let me have it. As I grew older, I came to know that although it's merely a figure of speech, no truer words have been spoken as it relates to describing individual struggles in life and the gifts that come from them.

Recently, I was going through a challenging situation. I felt overwhelmed and found myself on the highway sobbing. If you don't get anything else from this book, please note that driving on any road crying is a bad idea, but driving on a California highway is just madness. Nevertheless, there I was with blurry eyes, a snotty upper lip and wet salty cheeks - very attractive.

I was 20 minutes into the drive and I had replayed the issue in my mind about 60 times, when I decided that I'd tortured myself enough. I took a deep breath and regained my composure. Although my eyes were still blurry, I caught a glimpse of the powder blue sky and perfectly fluffy clouds. A few seconds later the Goodyear Blimp floated overhead and I went absolutely nuts. The sobbing began again, but this time, I was crying tears of joy.

You see, for many years, I have been fascinated with the blimp. I had never seen it in person until I moved to Los Angeles. Without fail, it's brought me joy every time I've seen it. I can only assume that it connects with my spirit because it floats so easy over all the turmoil on the ground or maybe because it looks like a partially deflated football. For whatever reason, my heart bubbled with joy and excitement. I needed a sign of great things to come and there it was floating over my brokenness.

The blimp sighting reminded me that there is a blessing in the storm. Great things are happening around us all the time, even in our darkest moments. We just have to take a deep breath, regain our composure and open our eyes as much as possible to see them. Seeing the blimp moved me from a moment of self-pity and pain to one of gratitude. As a new set of tears ran down my cheeks, I began to quietly say, "thank you," over and over again. I ran down a mental list of all the things for which I was thankful. There was no way to get through every one of them, but for me that represented how small the issue was in comparison to all of the amazing gifts.

My blessing in the storm was a return to gratitude, but yours may be something completely different. You may find the love of your life because you had the courage to let go of a toxic relationship. You may start your own business because you were laid off from a job. You may write a best selling book because some challenge you faced gave you an expertise in overcoming! I promise something is there for you; you just have to have the mindset to focus on finding it.

The Structure of Challenges

When you consider the challenges you've faced in your life, think for a moment about the make up of each one. First, an issue appears. Most of them start out small and in some cases so small that you don't even realize it's an issue until later. You either try to resolve it or ignore it. If an issue moves into the challenge phase that means it wasn't resolved immediately.

Here is where things get a little sticky. Every one of us has an internal panic button. We hit it when we begin to feel the sensation of being overwhelmed. Some tend to hit it very quickly, while others don't become alarmed until a situation is a full-fledged crisis. The range can be as drastic as some people coughing two times and assuming they have pneumonia while others avoid going to the doctor even when they've been ill for months.

Back in 2004, my father was diagnosed with colon cancer. Less than a year later, he was gone. While cancer can move very aggressively in a short period of time, we discovered during his initial diagnosis that he'd likely been living with the disease for 10 or 15 years.

The clues were absolutely there that something was wrong, but rather than get himself checked out, he ignored the symptoms and figured out a way to manage the pain.

Right away, I assumed that his panic button was broken. After the shock of the diagnosis dissipated, I realized that his response to the overwhelming feeling was to ignore it. My dad had been a part of his dad's battle against prostate cancer. I was still in the womb when his father passed away, but I distinctly remember dad's stories about how difficult it was to see my grandfather suffering. I am sure this is the fate he wanted to avoid the most. In his panic, he never sought treatment.

The most important lesson about challenges is that they don't go away. Issues can disappear, but challenges left unattended only grow in magnitude. You will have to deal with the situations that overwhelm you one way or another. Depending on the circumstance, they can take on the growth pattern of cancer in your life. One day, there are only a few small cells of this challenge, then over time you re-examine and see that it's a mass.

The good news is that every challenge is treatable. The trick is to catch it early and to appropriately respond when your panic button is activated. No matter how the challenge began, if it's your challenge - it's YOUR challenge. Another person may have been central to the development of the issue, but you are 100% responsible for moving yourself toward a resolution. My dad didn't run out to the cancer store and buy a six-pack of malignant cells. He did, however, smoke cigarettes for many years and had a diet that consisted of lots of processed meat. He didn't have regular check ups or get a tremendous amount of exercise. When his internal panic button went off, he chose to ignore it.

Some of you will feel a little bit of outrage rumble up in your system and attempt to attack my personal responsibility argument. You will cite examples of situations where completely innocent people who were extremely responsible got hit with a challenge that was out of their control. My response to you, once again, is that no matter how or why the challenge is introduced, once it's yours - it's YOURS.

I get that it's a bitter pill to swallow. I've had to swallow it on more occasions than I care to share. I can assure you though, once you own the challenge, whether you feel it's fair or unfair, you have the power to overcome it. Living in a state of denial prevents you from taking charge of your experience. It places you at the mercy of the challenge with no recourse. Owning the challenge empowers you to completely change your circumstances regardless of what they are.

While acknowledging and owning your challenge is the first step to overcoming it, this isn't the last step. You have to create a plan of attack that starts immediately. You must know that you deserve to have health and happiness and that the sacrifices you make to ensure that happens are absolutely worth it. Your dedication to a great life should be as serious as when a couple commits to marriage vows. The positive way you carry out your day should be for better or for worse, in sickness and in health. Your attitude and commitment to dealing with your challenges makes all the difference in the world.

Thank You Unthinkable

This year, I had several close friends lose their jobs unexpectedly. Each of the situations unfolded differently and their outlook on the job loss was dissimilar as well. The range of emotions went from shock and disappointment to relief and joy. Regardless of their initial feeling, everyone experienced some fear. Even when you hate your job, you'd rather be in the position of letting go of it instead of it letting go of you. When you let go of your job, you also want to be sure to have a great job to replace it.

This wasn't the case for my friends. While I mentioned each of them had very different circumstances surrounding their departures, they all had one important commonality. Each needed to leave in order to get back on track with their pursuit of a fulfilled life. All had been secretly and sometimes not so secretly job searching. Anytime we'd communicate, they complained about their jobs. If they saw a way to depart prior to the unthinkable happening, they would have. Unfortunately, the comfort of a paycheck kept them locked in way longer than they should have been.

In many cases, being comfortable can be an extremely dangerous situation. It will keep us in a position to accept less than we're worth in relationships and jobs. We are programmed to focus more on loss than gain. The ironic element of this is just beyond the perceived loss is infinite gain.

When I think of how we process potential losses, I often view it in terms of the game show "Let's Make a Deal." The premise of the game is that contestants must make deals for prizes, some of which can be seen immediately and some that remain a mystery until after the deal is made. Contestants feel an adrenaline rush as they consider trading the prize they currently have for one that is completely unknown. They look around to audience members for reassurance. Sometimes they even silently pray for direction.

A lot of energy is directed toward making a choice. Ultimately, there are only two potential outcomes: 1. receiving a prize or 2. receiving no prize, but walking away having had a once in a lifetime game show experience. The sweaty palm, lip biting, hand wringing contestants ride a wave of emotions before making a decision where the only thing they could lose is something they didn't have prior to the show. There is no real loss.

When you consider your blessing in the storm, understand that losses and gains are merely a matter of perception. The truth is that we receive gifts every single minute of the day, but when life is peachy, we tend not to acknowledge them. We take them as givens and move on with our daily tasks. However, when a challenge causes us to redirect our attention, something as small as a blimp sighting can mean the world to us.

8 ONCE YOU KNOW YOU – GROW YOU

For the most part, the previous chapters have been about figuring yourself out. We've explored the things that hold you back as well as what will make you great. This is a never-ending, lifelong process. You should be discovering new details about yourself everyday as well as remembering old ones. Please note that not everything you discover or re-discover is designed for you to pursue as a large-scale passion project or financial opportunity. Those endeavors will certainly set themselves apart, as you will feel a different level of excitement when you think of them. Trust your gut! It will help you distinguish a business venture from a hobby.

Hobbies and Happies

Several years ago, my mom retired from the education field after 40 years of service. She taught elementary school music in Virginia for 30 years and then dedicated another ten years of sharing her musical and developmental talents with students in North Carolina. She is absolutely beloved by her former students and colleagues in my hometown.

Toward the latter part of her career, mom's work began to evolve. While many teachers her age steered clear of incorporating new technology in their lesson planning, my mom jumped at the opportunity. She took classes, bought equipment and applications and read lots of material all in an effort to share these advancements with her students. Although she would never call herself an overall expert, she has become an expert in her circle of friends. Mom is the go to person whenever someone needs a device set up or presentation developed.

Over the years as her interest and skill in this area has grown, people have talked to her about starting a small business providing technical support. Time and time again she has shot down the idea. Mom just likes helping people without the pressure of generating revenue from her activities. A simple thank you is a sufficient reward for her. She has made a conscious decision that her enthusiasm for technology will never grow past the realm of a hobby and that's just fine.

Hobbies are wonderful all by themselves. Some of them can become income generating while others can disappear altogether. As your life evolves, so will the activities that make up your day. This doesn't give you license to be a flake. When you make a full commitment to a higher-level item on your list, you should see it through until the end. However, you will have plenty of lower level items to come and go.

For example, last time I was in Las Vegas, I drooled whenever I passed by the Black Jack table. I wanted to play just for the heck of it, but I hadn't been at a table since I was in graduate school. I wrote, "re-learn Black Jack" in my journal. I will definitely get to it and win some money at the table, but my goal is not to become a professional. I wouldn't categorize it as an income generating opportunity or even a hobby, but rather, a *happy*.

Happies are activities you take on for a short period of time because they bring you enjoyment and when you are done, you move on. You can re-visit *happies* at anytime. There is no real commitment required and no cancellation fees.

Growth Opportunities

So *happies* are activities you enjoy for a moment and hobbies are ones that you enjoy for an extended period of time without the expectation of financial reward. Growth opportunities, however, are a completely different category of activity. These are the passion projects that require you to stretch yourself. I call them growth opportunities for two reasons - you will grow them in addition to them growing you.

Growth opportunities typically have the potential to change the financial landscape of your life. They can gain you notoriety or position you as an expert in a given field, if you so desire. Growth opportunities are not, however, jobs. They can create space for advancement within existing career fields or assist with a transition to a new industry. They can also be developed into entrepreneurial endeavors. The only limitations set for growth opportunities are the ones you place on them.

Over the course of my life, I worked in several different industries. The vast part of my professional experience, though, has come from the higher education field. I felt a strong connection to student affairs work during my college years and even worked in several different support offices as an undergrad. Quite a few of my college mentors steered me in the direction of continuing the work in some capacity. While I didn't exactly know how I would, I decided to pursue it as an option after graduate school.

My first professional job in the field was as a Residence Hall Director at Cornell University, where I had received my master's degree two years prior. I instantly fell in love with mentoring students. I didn't have an academic background in Student Development, but I learned some theories along the way. My area of expertise was more related to the manner in which I could naturally develop a genuine relationship with my students. More than anything, I wanted them to succeed and I was excited to coach them through their journey.

I remained in Residence Life for many years, but it wasn't because housing in and of itself was a huge passion of mine. I enjoyed the work because it gave me a chance to use my experiences for the benefit of others. That work eventually spread beyond student life. Over the past few years, I've helped scores of colleagues and clients successfully maneuver through job searches and life changes.

The growth opportunity started very simply as a desire to help students. It took on many forms over the years until a specific area of expertise within that broad field was born. Today, I consider myself to be a success coach. I work with individuals and groups to help them tap into their full potential, see beyond their current circumstances and create their desired life. This book happens to be one component of that larger life endeavor.

Finding Your Growth Opportunity

Finding your growth opportunity begins with you tapping into what's truly important. This is not an overly complicated yearlong voyage into the abyss of your soul. It starts with asking some simple questions and noting the first answer that comes to mind. I repeat - the first answer that rises to the surface must be documented. We've become so accustomed to dismissing our initial responses in an effort to locate "appropriate" ones that rarely do we connect with our true thoughts.

Below is a list of idea generators you can use to help you identify potential growth opportunities or remind you of ones you've forgotten. Even if you are absolutely sure you already know what you want to pursue, go through the list to gain further insight.

Self-Check

1. If money were not a factor, what would I do everyday?

2. When I _____, I'm always happy.

3. I always dreamed of being a _____.

4. I want to do more_____ and less _____ everyday.

5. If I were campaigning for political office, my platform would be based on these key components _____.

6. I don't agree with the _____ law (or policy at work) and _____ is what I'd do to change it.

7. _____ is a problem I'd like to solve and here's how I'd do it _____. (Be sure to focus on the idea and not all the details related to doing it.)

8. As the CEO of my life, the most important skills I bring to the table are _____.

9. If called to the stand as an expert witness in a court case, my testimony would reflect my knowledge of _____.

10. I'd love to study _____.

Look over your notes and feel the positive energy from your ideas as it leaps off the page. This unique and special list is not like anyone else's. Even if you found someone who had similar interests, you would be approaching these passions from a completely different perspective. Your list has your genetic coding. It is an extension of you.

If you were lazy and didn't put your responses on paper, don't go any further until you do. You cannot risk having your notes live solely in the jungle of your head. Surely, it will not survive battling against grocery lists, work projects, play dates, sports scores, deadlines, etc.

You should be able to put your hands on this paper at any time, just in case new information surfaces that you need to document. These notes also serve as a reminder that there are possibilities beyond your current circumstances.

9 WHEN BUTS ATTACK

Have you ever had a brilliant idea that you knew would make you millions, change your life or solve a complex common problem? Perhaps your idea wasn't a "change the world" type of concept, but maybe just an innovative way to improve a system at your job. Regardless of the magnitude or scope of it, I am certain that most of you have had at least one great idea pop up in your mind. Many of you have a list of them. And if you're like me, you have notebooks, scrap paper, computer files, electronic phone notes and cocktail napkins with tons of inventions, innovations, concepts and cures.

Whether for a split second or a lifetime, that idea occupied a space in the dream file cabinet of your mind. Some were filed in the "wouldn't it be great?" section where spur of the moment ideas are generated. Others were filed in the "to be tackled when" section where amazing ideas go that can't be accomplished in the moment. The "to be tackled when" file is filled with ideas that you believe require more money, time or expertise than you have at the date of the filing. Regardless of where these ideas land in the cabinet, most go there to die.

Unfortunately, we live in a society that gives a lot of lip service about supporting dreams, but in actuality, creates many structural barriers that limit our ability to manifest them on a full-time basis. A few bold, hardheaded people charge through the barricades of tradition to pursue their dreams without restraint. The rest of us settle for reaching small dreams. Even then, many of the small dreams are watered down versions of a much greater initial vision. You may have dreamed of developing some incredible nautical innovation, but instead settled for owning a boat.

Responsibility Blues

Why does this have to be? Well, we live in a society that promotes the idea of responsibility. Being responsible is defined as having an obligation to do something, or having control over or care for someone, as part of one's job or role. There is nothing about the denotation of the word that contributes to the slaughter of hundreds of thousands of dreams everyday, but rather the connotation that has the blood of dreams on its hands.

When we think about responsible people, they typically have similar character traits. The first is, they have a job and/or they are acquiring the educational credentials to obtain a job. Interestingly, certain types of jobs or educational experiences are deemed as more responsible choices than others. Responsible people also have an appropriate amount of children at an appropriate time with an appropriate partner. They live in appropriate domiciles and pay bills and taxes by the prescribed deadlines.

I will leave it to social scientists and historians to share insights on how this came to be. The origin of these rules only matters to me as a point of fascination. I am most interested, however, in the fact that we buy into this model, lock, stock and barrel. Even those of us who live, in part, outside the model, pass it on generation after generation.

The system is ingenious because it is self-sustaining. This is due to the unyielding efforts of people who can never fully live within the guidelines. Our preoccupation with living acceptable lives by any means necessary, keeps us focused on being seen as responsible rather than creating a life formula that works best for us. We meticulously maintain the walls of the responsibility prison focusing all of our efforts on getting those bills paid before the deadline so our credit score remains in tact and we can buy the house in the good school district to ensure our kids get into a good college so they can find a good job that will help them pay their bills before the deadline.

Sheesh! It looks worse on paper than it did when it was just a thought rattling around in my head. Nevertheless, this system forces you into buying a file cabinet for all those magnificent dreams. There's no way in the world you can fit 100% into the responsibility mold and accomplish the truly courageous dreams locked away in your head and heart. Believe me, I've tried it on every level. In order to do something different, you really have to DO SOMETHING DIFFERENT.

Read any article or book about a person deemed as an innovator. Every story will have one common characteristic that has nothing to do with credit scores or college degrees. The tie that binds them all is they made a decision at a certain point to depart from tradition. They all made an "irresponsible" choice in order to make a life-changing discovery and build an empire from nothing.

Interestingly, there is not one story about the world's most responsible human being. There is no hall of fame for the people who never, ever paid a bill late. Nobel doesn't give out any prizes for perfect attendance. I take nothing away from people who follow up on their commitments. My question is why we don't feel like we have a say in the creation of those commitments? Furthermore, why don't those commitments ever involve us thinking or living outside the box?

Resuscitating Your Dreams

Developing a new way of being that best suits your personal needs and desires does not mean you should do the opposite of what is defined as responsible. That strategy still keeps the existing structure as the ruling force in your life. You will essentially be making decisions based on the very thing you wish to escape. Instead, your first agenda item should involve you continuing the soul-searching work you started at the beginning of this book. It's important that you understand what you ultimately want before executing a plan.

Once you have some starter ideas, create a vision board that reflects your true interests. Please note as always, interests and desires can change over time. Don't beat yourself up if you begin moving toward life as a treasure hunter when you discover your passion for service work. The "responsible" person's code is to identify one profession and stick with it. If that doesn't work for you, it's okay. The point is to give yourself the mental, physical and emotional flexibility to be your true and authentic self.

Break into that dream file cabinet and begin to connect the dots between your previous ideas and the new life you plan to develop. You will be quite surprised at how strong connections exist between the dreams you've had all along and your current thought process. The reason everything melds together perfectly is because it all comes from the same incredibly beautiful place - inside you.

Now the real work is about to begin. Once you've started your break with tradition and are forging ahead with building at least one of your dreams, you will meet the dreaded resistance. This is the place where many brave pioneers tuck their tails and run. I will admit I have been there more than once. A discouraging word from a trusted friend or relative, poor initial results on a project launch or even the fear of these outcomes can land a dream in the "mission aborted" file, never to be seen again.

Remember failure is a part of every success story. The Wright Brothers didn't decide they wanted to fly on day one and by day two were soaring high above the clouds in the cockpit of a 747. It was a process for them, just as it will be for you. You will experiment with different strategies to achieve your goals. Some ideas will be hugely successful, while others will be flops.

Some years ago, when I first moved to Detroit, I decided to get into the cosmetic network marketing industry. I became an independent representative for an excellent company with wonderful products and an inspiring company history. I had never done anything like it before, but I jumped in headfirst and purchased $1200 worth of products to get my business off the ground quickly. A few failed sales pitches in and I retreated into my shell. I quit the business and gifted family and friends my remaining product inventory as birthday and holiday presents.

Many years passed and because of my failure, which was due 100% to my lack of commitment, I became an anti-network marketing spokesperson. Anyone who approached me with a system got a hard "no." I was brutal. Several months ago, however, my partner and I met a former Warner Brothers employee named Karika who introduced us to another concept within the industry. The old "you failed at that" message darted through my mind. I was completely closed off, but Karika didn't give up on providing us with the company and industry facts and figures.

After looking at the idea with an open mind, it was clear that this could be a game changer. The irony was magnificent as I shared the concept with friends and family members who had once bashed network marketing alongside me. This time around, I didn't fold after a few "nos" and a few avoided calls. I was much stronger in how I felt about myself and what I was sharing. As a result, we immediately found success. We've been having an incredible time building a business that will sustain us for the rest of our lives.

I can't help but to wonder, if I were in a better place in my own personal development years ago if I would have achieved the level of success in the first network marketing venture as I have in this one. While I will clearly never know, I am so grateful for second chances. Life is not about being perfect - it's about perfecting. You won't get everything right all the time, but you learn from each circumstance and apply those lessons to future situations.

Once you've overcome your personal fears and the need for those around you to accept your path, you will be able to do anything. Fear is the number one reason why dreams die in the file cabinet. You may have a laundry list of excuses about why your plan didn't work, but the majority of them are rooted in fear. Hesitation, lack of commitment and decision paralysis are all fear-based challenges.

An obvious excuse we often use to explain failure is a lack of money. More often than not, the root of this issue is also fear-based. The first question to ask as a checkpoint for this is, "when pursuing the dream at hand, did you fully commit to securing the necessary resources to make the endeavor possible?" The quick answer may be "yes," but the real answer is "probably not." Full commitment to a growth opportunity means that you went into asset liquidation mode, asked that relative you never speak to for a bridge loan or started collecting aluminum cans for extra cash. If any of that seems like too much, it means that you weren't fully committed. Underneath it all, the lack of commitment stems from the fear that if you go all in and it doesn't work, you'll look like a fool and/or lose whatever you currently have.

A few months ago, I watched an inspiring video posted on social media by an actor, model and musician who happens to be a part of one of the largest action movie franchises in history. In the video, Tyrese Gibson explains how in order to make his dreams a reality; he collected and returned shopping carts for one quarter apiece. He spent full days in the parking lots of grocery stores, often shunned by store patrons. He was doing honest work, hustling the best way he knew how. Now, he has access to a lifestyle that affords him the ability to have a personal shopper. He fully committed to a vision and now enjoys the reward.

The great news is that those of us who break thru the barrier of fear can have everything the universe has to offer. We can open our file cabinets and manifest dream after dream after dream without limitations. We can cure diseases, end poverty, travel to outer space or simply spend our days on a beach hammock writing poetry. It matters less about what the dream is and more about the commitment we have to achieve it.

10 BUT BUSTERS

While this book is meant to be fun, the work to get you to your heaven on earth is not easy. My tear stained pillow could tell you stories. During my coaching sessions, sometimes I encourage people to have a nice ugly cry. We focus so much energy on presenting a great face that we ignore the chaos and confusion bubbling inside of us. When I start to feel overwhelmed, I will sometimes trigger a cry by listening to several Sade songs back to back. She can really get a good cry kick started. Sometimes only a few bars in I let it rip until I look so ridiculous that I have to laugh. I, then, blow my nose, clean my face and get back to business.

When you're on a mission, there's no time for long, drawn out pity parties. Have a short, expressive one with the musical artist of your choice then move forward. Your invention is waiting to be designed, your business is waiting to be launched and your family is waiting for you to stop sobbing in the bathroom so they can use it.

In addition to my short cry party tip, I have several others to help you bust the *buts* you will come up against.

Accountability Buddy

Find an accountability buddy immediately. This is a person who is also working toward a challenging goal and one whom you trust. Every week, you need to make contact with your buddy. As much as possible, try to keep each other in a positive frame of mind, but be prepared to be a good listener when the fertilizer hits the fan in your buddy's life.

My friend Candace has been my accountability buddy for years. I hesitated to even mention her name in the book, because if she were ever approached with a big enough wad of cash as a payment to share my vulnerabilities, I'd be in trouble. Almost everyday during the book writing process, I've been in touch with her. We send each other inspiring text messages, share accomplishments and do a lot of venting. When I have the urge to throw up my hands and quit, she kicks my *but* and when she gets overly stressed about her dissertation, I kick hers.

Play

Take time out from your dream-making to play. Rhonda Byrne's recommends this in her book; *The Power* and I definitely incorporate it into my daily routine. While I greatly enjoy going to the beach, the movies and to the amusement park, it's not always an option. Time is not readily available for several hours or several days of play, but a few minutes every few hours is doable. My secret is "Peanut Butter Jelly Time." I dance around the house to it multiple times a day. My poor partner, Joe, just looks at me and shakes his head. I'm sure he wishes I had another theme song to be completely silly to, but that's my pick.

Find something silly you can do for a few minutes of the day. The stress you will relieve during that time will help you power through your empire building tasks. It will also keep the *but* of exhaustion at bay.

Heroes and Mentors

You definitely want to be in the company of people who inspire you. Even though you may not actually meet all of these people, connect to them through their words and accomplishments. If you have access to video footage, articles, scriptures, mementos, etc, use those items to feel their presence.

Some mornings when I feel a little unproductive, I'll watch several clips of Tony Robbins or Eric Thomas. After a few minutes of their high-energy direction, I transition into beast mode. I know I can tackle the day with an extreme amount of force. If I need a more soothing and affirming moment of inspiration, I call on Oprah. No one, in my opinion is better at putting things into perspective.

Whenever possible, it's great to have mentors you can learn from face to face. Melvin, Shelley, Dave and Yvette are my mentors in LA. Each serves a very important and specific purpose in my life. I listen closely to their instruction. I study their movements and I use the knowledge they share to make adjustments in my own life.

When identifying mentors, be sure to select people who have achieved a level of success you aspire to achieve. Don't waste your time searching for perfect people as they don't exist, but rather find ones who shine through their imperfections. Great mentors are transparent about their *buts*, so you can learn some real strategies for overcoming yours.

Use Your Imagination

Several times a day, I imagine myself in the place I aspire to ultimately be. This is not to suggest I am unhappy with where I am currently. I am merely charting the path to my next destination. Since I don't have precise directions to this place, I focus my energy on knowing exactly what the destination looks like. I see everything in vivid, high definition detail. I even know the sound of my pocket dog's tiny footsteps on the hardwood floors.

Acquaint yourself with the lifestyle you are working toward. When it seems like nothing is going right with your plan, imagine taking your family to their new home, going on the dream vacation you always wanted and accepting the Nobel Prize for the dynamic contributions you made to your field. This exercise can quiet the *but* of "it's taking too long" or "I'm not good enough."

No Matter What, Focus on the Goal

No one can prepare you for what you may come against once you've made a full commitment to your growth opportunity. I can assure you that the bigger your dream is, the bigger the opposition will be. And while it is easy to think the world is simply against you, the truth is that the world is preparing you. Whatever challenges you face are for refining purposes only.

This transformation is personal for you, but as best as you can, don't take the attacks on your character or your dream personally. Remain focused at all times on the goal and not the stumbling blocks that are on the path to it. When you direct your attention to a stumbling block, your destination becomes the stumbling block. Your energy and effort will go into managing an endeavor that has nothing to do with your desired life. As a matter of fact, it is the very opposite of what you desire.

Criticism can often send you into an unproductive place. Before you become unhinged, learn to recognize the difference between people who are sharing constructive criticisms and those who are maliciously attacking you. A comment shared with you in the spirit of helping you move forward is not someone "hating on you." However, when you are certain that a person is acting out of malice, don't waste time crafting an equally malicious response. Realize that your goal has nothing to do with them, but their goal has everything to do with you. They're investing time and energy into tearing you down, which means their not building anything in their lives. Let them exhaust themselves while you smile and keep laying bricks.

Don't fall prey to "*but* people are hating on me." Who cares? Be concerned if there's no resistance. If no one is talking about you, then you must not be kicking up enough dust. When people are talking about you, no matter how awful their comments, take it as a compliment. You are significant to them!

Find an Example Then Be One

Earlier, I encouraged you to identify heroes and mentors who can inspire you throughout your journey. It is also important to find someone with whom you can identify who has achieved greatness or someone who has made significant contributions to your desired industry. The best-case scenario is to find one person who fits into both categories. Use him/her as an example for what you, too, can achieve.

I encourage people to do this because it's important to see what's possible. Sometimes we need to know "if they can do it, I can do it." Many overcame the same *buts* you must overcome. When you feel like you're getting stumped by a pretty hefty *but*, find inspiration in a success story of a kindred spirit.

Be prepared that at a certain point you will be the example for someone else. Wear that badge with honor. Share your story as much as you can with people who can benefit from your tale of transformation. Keep a diary of the wonderful moments and the heartbreaks. Your journey is not just for you. It is for those who will build on what you establish.

Be Resourceful

Unfortunately, much of what we've learned in life encourages us to direct our attention toward lack. When starting this daring journey to an optimal life, you must shift your way of thinking to focus on abundance. This can be difficult when it seems necessary to have a particular item currently not in your possession. Let's be real, most of the time - it's money. Our lazy minds shut down when we see our bank account can't support a critical transaction. Immediately we go into, "I would, *but* I don't have enough money."

A resourceful mind, however, starts the process of finding out how it can secure the money to move forward. My senior year of college, several of my closest friends and I decided to make the most of our last spring break at Guilford and go on a fantastic trip. We were excited about getting away together for one last hoorah. There was only one problem with our plan - we were broke.

Keisha, Nina, Veronica and I sat around a table in the dining hall brainstorming potential escape plans and strategies to finance them. I'm not certain who came up with the idea of a yard sale, but it was ingenious. We dug into our closets as well as the closets of nearby friends and relatives. We created a marketing campaign for our "Yard Sale EXTRAVAGANZA" and we developed a pricing plan for our merchandise.

Our budget for the whole event was $20, so at the end of the night when we counted the profits, we were over the moon excited. We brought in over $600, which covered our accommodations for our Bahamian spring break adventure.

You don't need a stock pile of cash to start working on a growth opportunity. All you need is an open mind. The ideas and people you need to get you to the necessary capital will appear if you truly activate your mind. Don't let the lack of resources *but* keep you from accessing unlimited resources.

Pay It Forward

When you contribute to the success of others, the universe returns the favor. You should never give with the expectation of receiving, but just know that it is a guaranteed outcome. Giving is not limited to financial contributions. Sometimes when we encounter a person who has achieved great wealth, we think they don't want for anything. Anyone you come across, regardless of his or her financial status can benefit from the gift of a smile or a kind word.

One summer when I was in college, I returned to my room after a long day at work. I was pretty tired and planned to take a nap, but saw my voicemail light was on. I had one message from a complete stranger. He said he was having a horrible day and accidentally dialed my number. My chipper greeting on the voicemail brightened his day. He thanked me, then ended the call.

I listened to the message twice and suddenly I wasn't so tired. It reminded me that being positive, even while doing something seemingly insignificant like recording a voicemail greeting could make an impact on someone's life. Knowing that I brightened someone's day brightened my day.

Imagine what your impact can be when you intentionally lend a hand, share your resources or write a positive review for a brand new business in your neighborhood. The great feeling is something nobody and no *but* can take away.

11 BUY YOUR OWN STOCK

For whatever reason we are a society fascinated with what everyone else has. We started out trying to keep up with the Joneses and now we're trying to keep up with the Kardashians too. Sometimes we unknowingly base our dreams on the lifestyles of others. Those of us who have not discovered our true selves and true passions can spend a lifetime following the lead of other wayward journeymen.

Before I started taking personal responsibility for my life choices, I found great scapegoats for this in the media and corporate America. I argued in my most assertive angry voice, "They are shoving their options down our throats and they make us slaves to jobs in an effort to sell us lives they construct for magazine ads." The truth is that there are marketing gurus hired by every organization from Congress to Coca-Cola with the specific purpose of shifting and shaping our perspectives. However, in all things, we have choices. There are only a few situations I can think of where the, "I was forced to do it," argument can be made. It is the exception and not the rule in connection with this topic.

In addition to buying other people's lifestyles, we also buy other people's wisdom. We believe that company executives know so much more than we do on the ground. Even when we question their decision-making and integrity, we still feel somehow, that we are far removed from that position. Sometimes we'll huddle up with friends and co-workers to talk about what we'd do if we were in their place, but the reality is that most of us would scurry away from such a role.

The world's best and worst business and political leaders wake up every morning knowing that they must make decisions that have major implications on the state of a company, industry, country and/or world. In our heart of hearts, the majority of us don't want to take on such significant tasks. No matter how opinionated we might be, most people would rather follow than lead. It's safer to be able to critique from the sidelines.

The system is set in place - others decide and we respond. The responders make up the majority and ultimately become totally immersed in a passive existence. The mind numbs and the body operates on autopilot when directed by leaders. Even when it feels wrong and completely counter to everything we need and desire, we cannot do anything but follow. We question our instincts and begin to rely on outside information from "experts" to direct our paths.

When sharing the concept of my network marketing company, I often have people tell me they have to do some research. I begin to chuckle a bit, because I know their research will go no farther than what they can discover in a quick Internet search. While the Internet is an amazing resource for housing a plethora of information, that does not mean all information suppliers are credible. Almost everyday, I come across a celebrity death hoax on the net, yet this is the place where the average person researches a business opportunity. I shake my head when I think about a society of people who will trust the opinions of anyone with a laptop and wifi.

So we spend our days watching other people take action and we wait for their decisions to be passed down to us. Many of us never seize the opportunity to get into the driver's seat of our lives. However, it is only then, when we take complete control over our activities and success, that we will begin to discover a glorious life. Instead of buying stock in the opinions and lifestyles of others, we must buy our own.

Start Buying

Based on the exercise in Chapter 8, you should have identified at least one growth opportunity to pursue. Now start buying up your stock! I know that sounds strange, but everyday you need to purchase stock in your idea, invention, passion or life change. The currency you will use is time and positive affirmations. You need to invest as much as you possibly can into the YOU Corporation. Every single day, you must invest regardless of what's going on in your life.

When it comes to investing in YOU Corp, it will be very easy to use the "I don't have enough time" *but* to excuse away inactivity. Often being tied up with children, aging parents, jobs, other community and household obligations, school and even long commutes make excellent excuses not to make the daily investment. They are all important and real challenges that people face, but they are still not legitimate reasons to shirk your investments.

The reality is, there are more activities in our lives than we'd like to admit that have very little value in the grand scheme of what we're trying to accomplish. If you are not someone who makes a living or hopes to make a living utilizing social media, then there's no reason for you to spend 2 hours a day scrolling through status updates and pictures. If you check your pages ten times a day for about fifteen minutes, you've spent over 2 hours liking pictures of cats, babies and scenery. Cutting your total time to 20 minutes a day would help you invest more in YOU Corp.

By simply changing your social media, television, web browsing and sleep habits, you can find a sweet cache of time to invest in something that will pay dividends. Some will have to be more creative than others. You may have to rely on listening to audio books instead of music when you commute or exercise. You may have to remove social media apps or at the very least notifications from your phone to prevent constant distractions. You may even have to sacrifice cable television. Find the time to invest, by any means necessary. I promise YOU're worth it.

Using daily affirmations as currency is another key and critical component to your investment strategy. Overhauling your life requires you to go head to head with old thinking. All the *buts* you're holding onto function solely to slow your progress. Not only must you eliminate them from your thought process, but also replace them with affirming thoughts. For example, if you are like me, you've failed at a previous business venture. When memories of that failure arise and create new anxiety, I shut off those thoughts immediately and replace them with "I am a smart, savvy and successful businesswoman." Eventually, my mind will get the hint and the negative way of thinking will fade away.

The Frien-emesis

Old thinking will not be your only nemesis. Other people may share negative opinions about what you are trying to accomplish. Don't be surprised if loved ones are among the group least supportive of your endeavors. I call an individual like this a *frien-emesis* as he/she is a friend and a nemesis all rolled up into one. While it may hurt, this is no time to let a *frien-emesis* slow your momentum. He or she is only operating from his or her own reality. Your *frien-emeses'* fears and lack of understanding fuel their dismissal of your passion. Sometimes their motive is to protect you from failure, but understand that if you have committed to a process, you should absolutely continue investing in YOU Corp. no matter what. Your commitment to the endeavor is all that counts.

I can think of several great ideas I abandoned after getting negative feedback from friends and family members. Now when I'm faced with those types of comments, I identify the information I can utilize for the betterment of the endeavor and then follow up with a silent affirmation. A critique can be an excellent tool to improve what you're doing and when coupled with an affirmation, you can use this moment to actually propel your work forward.

Mind YOUR Business

Just as caring too much about the opinions of others can derail you, becoming too concerned about what others are doing can throw you completely off course. Stop wasting time comparing your results with your peers. Remember that everyone starts his/her process with unique experience DNA that impacts how growth opportunities will develop. No two journeys will ever be the same as it relates to steps to success or timeframe.

Keep focused on what you're doing as this is of the utmost importance. Certainly utilize wise counsel to help you tweak your plan, but never expect to achieve results identical to theirs. Bob Proctor explains in his book, *It's Not About the Money* that even if someone mapped out every detail of his or her success strategy, you will not have the exact same experience.

Social media plays a huge factor in many individuals' perception of whether or not they size up to their peers. Prior to the launch of these sites and applications, we only had media access to celebrities and public figures. Now we can see just about everyone. As we sit in our cubicles waiting for five o'clock to roll around, we can see all of our friends who are on vacation, just came back from vacation or are about to go on vacation. All we can do is dream.

After checking out the 125th vacation photo, we are excited to see the "cats that knock over stuff" video or take a personality test to see which superhero we are most like. We want to be happy for others, but sometimes we become overwhelmed that we are not living the charmed life we imagined.

I was certainly in that position several years ago. Thanks to a few bold maneuvers and a great business opportunity, I'm living a highly fulfilled life, but back then I had a job from which I never felt I could step away. Even when I took a day off, I spent several late nights in the office before my departure date to prepare and knew I'd be doing the same when I returned from my break. I watched people online "Living la Vida Loca" while I was just feeling loco. At that time, I was fairly stationary and most days eating my weight in chips.

In the meantime, my friend Tiffany from high school was having a blast. She traveled. She worked out. She took pictures of her meals, which all looked like they came from a gourmet clean eating magazine. Admittedly, I started to wonder about my life choices. Tiffany was balling out of control and I was balled up on my couch eating out of an ice cream carton.

The answer to my problem was right there on the couch. I wasn't minding my business. I wasn't caring for myself mentally, physically or spiritually. How could I have a great life sitting on my butt and allowing my *buts* to takeover? When you mind your business, you get back to the first point I shared in Chapter 1 - you start living "this very minute." You take action no matter how deep you've been in the mire of foolishness.

I did that - eventually. Now, Tiffany is my body inspiration. She is a fitness guru who recently had a beautiful baby boy. Several days after her child's birth, she posted a picture of her stomach online. It's the one I've been dreaming of having - perfectly flat. I looked down at mine quietly resting on the top of my pants. It was almost as if it looked back at me, smiled and said, "One day, Nat…one day." I laughed hysterically before I got back to my writing project. Tiffany was minding her business, which is her physique and I was minding mine on my computer.

Because I am in a centered place, seeing someone achieve in an area where I have had limited success is not a bother. It is exciting to know the possibilities. I will get to the place I want to be one day and have access to an expert. The beauty of minding your business is that you become even more open to sharing and receiving than you ever were before. Your perspective shifts from, "I wish I could do that," to "I am excited to learn how she did it."

For those of you who have been thirsty for a sports metaphor, here you go. Life is a marathon, but it's yours alone to run. Your goal in the race is just to improve your time.

12 BUT PARALYSIS

You cleared away the mental clutter to identify your growth opportunity. You fully committed to the journey toward success. You bought a ton of your own stock and now - you're stuck. You don't know how. You don't know why, but you're at the gateway to the life you always dreamed of and you can hardly lift one foot in front of the other.

It happens to all of us at different points of the journey. Even after we've achieved a high level of success with a growth opportunity, we still can very easily slip into a state of paralysis. A financial snag, an unexpected life event, a crazy business associate or a lull in the process can send you spiraling. Just when you thought you had your *but* under control, it starts to take over - growing bigger and bigger and BIGGER everyday.

The worst of it is you know all of the steps to resolve the issue. You went through every one of them to start working on your growth opportunity in the first place. Although the sensible side of your mind is coaching you to keep calm and press on, the scared side is screaming, "run for the hills!"

The fear you experience once you've fully committed to your growth opportunity is far greater than when you are merely in the contemplation phase. At this point, your investment is public knowledge. Your friends and family know. They ask how things are going and you are certain, in your heart of hearts, that some of them are just waiting for you to fail. You don't want to give them the satisfaction, but you are so unsure of yourself at this point, it seems inevitable.

Now your *but* is enormous. It's taken over your life and you begin to plan your retreat. Your first thought is to go back to the last "comfortable" scenario. Perhaps you quit your job to start your own business and now you're scanning the job search sites and revising your resume. Maybe you decided to enroll in a four-year college and now you're thinking you should move into your parents' basement while you look for a full-time job.

Success Paralysis

Believe it or not, success can paralyze us as well. When we move into unfamiliar territory, our anxiety levels increase. This rule applies even if it's exactly where we hoped to be. What if we get everything we want and we just can't hold on to it? What if we ruin the best thing that's ever happened to us? What if we blow it?!?

This is why entertainers and other public figures struggle so much to constantly maintain their composure. The more eyes they believe are watching them, the more challenging it is to overcome the fear that their success is momentary. The celebrations in honor of their achievements are short lived as notables rush back to work looking for the next big project to keep the spotlight on. The pressure is tremendous and sometimes can be just too much to manage.

Fearing they can never top their last great offering, phenomenal actors step away from the set, talented musicians retire their metronomes and prolific writers fill up all the seating at the neighborhood coffee shop pretending to write, but all the while, playing "Words with Friends."

Bouncers

Some of us bounce to a new idea instead of fully retreating. When the excitement around one opportunity wanes, there's another waiting to capture our attention. We convince ourselves, it is the better deal and redirect our resources. When this happens, we never exert the same amount of energy as we did into the initial endeavor. We have to overcome the first hump of convincing ourselves that this in fact is the real deal.

How do I know this? I've lived it! When I was applying for college, I stated that my intended major was History. My plan was to become a high school Social Studies teacher and basketball coach. When I arrived on campus, I started taking classes in the business management major. I loved everything about it until I had my first Accounting class. Mind you, I needed to do well in two Accounting classes in order to satisfy the course requirements for a management degree. Since I had been a less than stellar student my first semester, I had no room for GPA error in order to keep my academic scholarship.

After the first quiz in my Accounting class, I was scrambling to find a drop slip for the course. Business management was not going to be an option that I could financially afford based on what I discovered from that first test. My GPA situation wouldn't jive with a C or a D. So while my understanding of the principles of accounting might have been horrible, my math was decent. I had to figure something out and quick.

I'd sold my family on all of these college majors and all I really needed was to lose my scholarship for them to know for certain that I was a flake. As soon as I dropped the Accounting class, I hallelujah danced all the way to my residence hall room. Once inside, I got down to business with a stack of note cards and a copy of the college catalog. I wrote down every class I had completed on a separate note card and spread the note cards out so I could see how I could match those classes with graduation requirements. I also thought about the classes I enjoyed most. I considered where I had the most success as it related to grades.

When I finished, I knew I would double major in African American Studies and Justice & Policy Studies. I felt positive about the decision and didn't feel any need to pitch the plan to anyone else. It was great because I had taken charge of my chaos and turned it into a strong choice.

The lesson here is that bouncing from one growth opportunity to the next can be very taxing. It's not the end of the world if you've been in that position, but to get out, you must stop for a moment to make a clear assessment of what you need to succeed. You may have to hold off on a project that you love doing in order to achieve the progress you desire. You will definitely have to rearrange your priorities, but isn't it worthwhile to at least have some inner peace about your process?

Saving Face - Leaving But

Once you're out of the state of paralysis and you're feeling good inside again, a little knot may turn up in your stomach if you have to explain to someone why your project came to a standstill or why you are on to something else. Even when a person approaches you to check in about life with the absolute best intentions, you might not be poised to discuss. In your mind you may take on the persona of a television reality star and begin a sassy neck roll, a finger wag followed by a snarky "none of your damn business." In truth though, you will likely fumble through a complicated explanation that makes you look as crazy as you previously felt. Just in case you need them, here are a few canned responses you can give to limit the pain of discussing a temporary setback.

Setback Comebacks:

1. Quite honestly, I had to update my plan of action to address current issues in the marketplace. That took some time, but it was worth the investment.

2. My vision is multi-layered, so I am always redeveloping the core components to create long-term success.

3. I find it difficult to turn down amazing opportunities, so I'm always in pursuit of new cutting edge ideas. I'm looking to be involved in the next Google!

Walk away from the exchange with your head up. Your conversation was with another imperfect human who has a *but* problem too. All of my heroes and sheroes have great stories of triumph and tragedy, amazing accomplishments and failed ventures, groundbreaking inventions and undeniable flops. That's what makes their stories spectacular and their successes real.

Remember that every experience in life is meaningful. Many of the lessons contained in this book came from missteps in my past. I could fill an encyclopedia set with boo boos and shenanigans of which I have been a part. I'm grateful for everything, because I am where I am as a result of the amazing decisions as well as the foolish ones.

13 BYE BUT

Saying good-bye to your *but* for good is extremely challenging. You've lived with your *but* for years. Some *buts* outlast spouses. The long-term relationship you've had with your *but* can't be eliminated in a day. It's a process!

If you have been a procrastinator most of your life, that *but* is just as much apart of you as the face you always make when you score a basketball shot. Even still, you have the power to change anything you desire with a bit of focused effort. The amount of energy you need to put toward the change should be in direct correlation to the length of time you've been plagued with that particular *but*.

Imagine if a new scientific study revealed that walking was unsafe and people all over the world were advised to hop instead. It would take some time to make the transition. However, if you truly believed your life was in danger as a result of continuing to walk, you'd hop right into hopping. You'd concentrate on making the change regardless of how challenging it might be. You must approach *but* elimination in this same regard. Your great life is in jeopardy every time you let your *but* take over.

"*But* no one will give me a shot," is a *but* that's been with me for years as it relates to my work as a screenwriter. My partner, Joe and I have had a bunch of near deals, but no real deals. Every week, we watch some of the most ridiculous television shows and movies on the planet and wonder how in the world they are funded while our projects are getting dusty on a shelf. "Wah, wah, wah!"

The most challenging part of the process is we've been in meeting after meeting about our projects where people share a great deal of enthusiasm over the material. "Wow, this is really great stuff!" "Love your style, love your humor!" When the meeting ends, we wait and wait and wait. When the phone rings, it's mom. When an e-mail arrives, it's Netflix letting me know about new release. Daggers!

Finally when we get back in touch with folks for an update, they hit us with a string of crazy *buts* that usually involve personal and family illnesses, unexpected extended vacations, deaths, dismemberments, natural disasters and sometimes a combination of a few.

We are not alone. When we speak with other people new to the business, they express the same woes. Instead of continuing to harbor the frustration of being locked out of the game, my partner and I decided we'd produce our own projects. "That will teach big, bad Hollywood a lesson," we thought. We got to work on a cost effective idea to utilize the resources at our disposal to create our own piece. Months of labor and a couple thousand dollars went into the production of a comedy website designed to help up and coming comedians gain exposure.

Our amazing plan hit several bumps in the road to production and even though we got a great prototype site up and running, it seemed like we were hamsters tumbling around on a big wheel. We had these great ideas, then no one to film them or great footage and no one to edit. We had access to great comedians at a time when no one was available to film or edit.

We decided to regroup again. In order for the project to work, we needed access to more resources, which put us back in the position of battling the "no one will give us a shot" *but*. I was *but* paralyzed for months. I whined a lot inside my head. After I tired of the pity party, I got back to business investing in myself. I restarted the personal development journey that had gotten me so close to getting everything I wanted in life.

One night after a busy day, I decided to meditate. I'd listened to an audio book by Russell Simmons a few months prior called, *Success Through Stillness* where he suggests repeating "rum" as a meditation mantra. I did it and after the urge to drink had passed, my spirit quieted. When I completed the meditation, I opened my eyes and the memory of this book idea reemerged after a year of laying dormant in my mind. It was something I could do without outside funding. I could self-publish it and finally, my work would be available for public consumption. The idea eliminated my *but*.

As inspired as I was to start the project, it still wasn't a breeze. Several nights I had aggressive writing plans mapped out, but instead I allowed "*but* let me watch this next episode of *The Real Housewives of Atlanta*," distract me instead of fully committing to the work. A few times, I got caught in the social media trap liking pictures and reading up on how I can lose up to five pounds drinking sassy water.

The process wasn't perfect because I wasn't perfect. I didn't allow the shame of my departure from focus throw me completely off track. I remembered my goal and re-directed my energy as soon as possible. I stayed up until 3:00 a.m. some nights making up for lost writing time, but I knew that sacrificing a little sleep for a short while was certainly worth the reward.

Below is one last self-check to help you close out the reading. If you've been doing the suggested activities throughout the book, you should have a better understanding of who you are and what you need to improve. The questions and statements in the self-check will help you remember discoveries and commitments you may have forgotten.

Self-Check

1. What is your biggest *BUT?*

2. Reflect on a time recently that you recognized your *but* was out and you were able to neutralize it.

3. What steps have you taken to lead a more centered life?

4. List at least one *happy*, hobby and growth opportunity you discovered or re-discovered as a result of this book.

5. Who are the heroes, mentors and examples you identified to motivate you and provide direction?

6. How are you paying it forward? What are you doing to invest in the success of others?

7. What have you changed about your schedule to ensure you can invest in YOU Corp. everyday?

8. How are you protecting yourself from *joy thieves?*

9. Have you recently experienced *but* paralysis? If so, how did you overcome it? If not, what is your plan of attack if you start to feel paralyzed?

10. What additional steps do you need to take to achieve your optimal results?

I pray that you will take the time to dig deep and identify the *buts* that have been sitting in the way of your progress. Your ideas and inventions can change life on our planet.

However, if you can't get passed your own excuses, those incredible visions will remain locked away in your dream file cabinet.

Remember that this very minute is all you have so use it wisely. Focus on becoming less self-centered and more centered. Be a *joy gifter* and not a *joy thief*. Invest in your own ideas rather than being dependent on the opinions of others and fight the urge to be a slave to responsibility. Stand up and claim the growth opportunities that will set you apart from everything you've ever known. No matter how many *buts* you have to kick, you are worth the fight.

So get off your butt right now and start overcoming your biggest *BUT!*

Made in the USA
Middletown, DE
02 July 2015